I have seen what possibility thinking has done for thousands of people just like you. I have watched all kinds of people face almost every conceivable situation. I have seen how the impossibility thinker is defeated every time. And I have also seen how the POSSIBILITY THINKER wins over seemingly impossible odds.

Why am I so sure this book can help you? Possibility thinking moved mountains in my personal life. I know it worked for me. If I communicate the principles to you it will work for you.

—Robert H. Schuller

ROBERT H. SCHULLER

MOVE AHEAD WITH POSSIBILITY THINKING

A JOVE BOOK

This Jove book contains the complete
text of the original hardcover edition.
It has been completely reset in a typeface
designed for easy reading, and was printed
from new film.

MOVE AHEAD WITH POSSIBILITY THINKING

A Jove Book / published by arrangement with
Doubleday & Company, Inc.

PRINTING HISTORY
Doubleday & Company edition published 1967

Fifteen previous paperback printings

Jove edition / November 1978
Ninth printing / June 1984

ISBN: 0-515-07935-9

Library of Congress Catalog Card Number: 7-15206

Jove books are published by The Berkley Publishing Group,
200 Madison Avenue, New York, N.Y. 10016.
The words "A JOVE BOOK" and the "J" with sunburst
are trademarks belonging to Jove Publications, Inc.

PRINTED IN THE UNITED STATES OF AMERICA

ACKNOWLEDGEMENTS

I am most grateful to:

The publishing companies which have permitted me to quote from the books indicated therein.

The ministers Norman Vincent Peale and Raymond J. Lindquist, who have done far more for me than they will ever know.

Our congregation of Garden Grove Community Church—the greatest collection of Possibility Thinkers I've ever known.

My wife, Arvella Schuller, and my friend, Stuart L. Daniels, for their invaluable advice and encouragement in the preparation of this book.

Dedicated to
my son
Robert Anthony Schuller
and to my daughters
Sheila Louise
Jeanne Anne
Carol Lynn
Gretchen Joy

CONTENTS

INTRODUCTION

By Dr. Norman Vincent Peale

I first met the author of this book when he invited me to visit his drive-in church in southern California more than ten years ago. At that time I was greatly impressed with the imagination, determination, and enthusiasm which had enabled him to face up to a seemingly impossible situation and find a solution. There had literally been no place for him to hold religious services in the community to which he had been assigned. The use of a drive-in theater for Sunday morning religious services was his answer.

Several years later I had the honor of participating in the ceremonies inaugurating a brand-new edifice—a beautiful walk-in drive-in church which Bob Schuller's ever fertile mind, unfailing enthusiasm and positive thinking had projected into reality.

Those qualities of mind and spirit which enabled one man to achieve his dream are communicated to the reader in this book. Principles and guidelines for achieving your own goals in life are given here. The reader is shown how to overcome the real and fancied roadblocks to personal progress and happiness by being a possibility thinker.

MOVE AHEAD WITH POSSIBILITY THINKING is an inspiring and deeply moving book, filled with great stories of inspiration. The religious message is woven into the exposition in a highly interesting and most attractive way. It is a highly readable and extraordinary human document which presents its message with economy of language.

I FOUND IT COMPLETELY FASCINATING!

I feel certain that any person who will read this book and act on it will be able to achieve anything he or she wants. I have read many books which offered inspiration and hope and presented positive programs for action. MOVE AHEAD WITH POSSIBILITY THINKING is one of the best.

I

IMPOSSIBILITY THINKERS
VS.
POSSIBILITY THINKERS

Are you   limping when you could be walking strong,
            whimpering when you could be whistling,
            crying when you could be laughing?
Are you   being defeated by your problems,
            facing frustrations that are discouraging you,
            heartaches that are depressing you?
Are you   bored with life,
            tired of living,
            lacking zest and excitement?
Are you   watching somebody make a
            great success of an opportunity you
            turned down?
Are your   projects and dreams
            struggling when they could be thriving,
            shrinking when they could be growing,
            failing when they could be succeeding?

THEN THIS BOOK IS FOR YOU!

This book is your chance to change your thinking and to change your life.

Speaking at Elmendorf Air Force Base in Anchorage, I was deeply impressed with the efficiency of the Alaskan Command. After a visit with the commander, General Raymond Reeves, I asked the officers at this

Top of the World base, "What is the secret of General Reeves' success?" The answers were summed up in a sentence: "The General is always telling us to 'stop thinking up reasons why something won't work and start thinking of ways in which we can make it work.'"

There are two basic types of thinkers within the human family. I choose to call these two types "possibility thinkers" and "impossibility thinkers." Which kind are you?

Many different species of birds fly along the California deserts. Some make wide circles in search of food and never find anything to eat. Then there is that inspiring miracle we call the California hummingbird. He jets over the wasteland and spots a bright flower blooming on a remote cactus. He dives down, spearing the blood-red heart of the sweet desert blossom, and drinks his honey. When others find nothing to eat, the hummingbird finds a flower. In his way, he is a possibility thinker.

THE IMPOSSIBILITY THINKERS

Impossibility thinkers are people who make swift, sweeping passes over a proposed idea, scanning it with a sharp negative eye, looking only for the distasteful aspects. They look for reasons why something won't work instead of visualizing ways in which it could work. So they are inclined to say "No" to a proposal, never giving the idea a fair hearing.

Impossibility thinkers are people who immediately, impulsively, instinctively, and impetuously react to any positive suggestion with a sweeping, unstudied, irresponsible assortment of reasons why it can't be done, or why it is a bad idea, or how someone else tried it and failed, or (and this is usually their clinching argument) how much it will cost! They are people who suffer from a perilous mental malignancy I call the impossibility complex. They are problem imaginators, failure predictors, trouble visualizers, obstacle envisioners, exaggerated-cost estimators.

Their attitude produces doubt, stimulates fear, and generates a mental climate of pessimism and fatigue. They are worry creators, optimism deflators, confidence squelchers. The end result? Positive ideas buried, dreams smashed, and projects torpedoed.

THE POSSIBILITY THINKERS

The possibility thinkers resemble the hummingbird that looks for and finds honey, often in the most unlikely and unthinkable places. The possibility thinkers perceptively probe every problem, proposal, and opportunity to discover the positive aspects present in almost every human situation.

They are people—just like you—who when faced with a mountain do not quit. They keep on striving until they climb over, find a pass through, tunnel underneath—or simply stay and turn their mountain into a gold mine.

WHY DO THEY SUCCEED?

They have trained themselves to look for the possibilities in all areas of life. They have learned how to:

- Overcome inferiority complexes and live confidently
- Listen to new ideas and evaluate them carefully
- Spot opportunities and seize them courageously
- Welcome challenging problems and solve them creatively
- Face personal tragedies with equanimity and, if possible, use them constructively

Great people!   These faith builders,
Hope boosters,
Confidence creators,
Enthusiasm generators,
Optimism spreaders!

History calls them:
Pace setters,
Record breakers.

Thank God for these dedicated dreamers,
these sanctified opportunists,
these glorified gamblers,
these powerful believers!

Just look at the inspiring monuments they leave behind them:

- Successful marriages and happy families
- Profitable businesses and great institutions
- Lifesaving drugs and surgical procedures
- Skyscrapers that stab steeply above the skyline
- Satellites that sail silently through the soundless sea of space
- Laughing children in homes made happy through the power of God's love

These are the monuments that remind us that possibility thinkers have passed this way.

This book is your invitation to become a POSSIBILITY THINKER and thus become a somebody in a world of too many nobodies, a success in a crowd of failures.

I promise you that if you will follow the principles of the possibility thinkers you, too, can

- turn dreams into exciting achievements
- turn problems into profitable projects
- turn obstacles into rare opportunities
- turn opportunities into rich enterprises
- turn tragedies into inspiring triumphs

Within these pages is the pathway to success. Follow this path carefully and your life will take on amazing new power.

WHY AM I SO SURE?

I have seen what possibility thinking has done for thousands of people just like you. As the pastor of one of the nation's largest churches, I have watched all kinds of people face almost every conceivable situation. I have seen how the impossibility thinker is defeated every time. And I have also seen how the POSSIBILITY THINKER often wins over seemingly impossible odds.

Why am I so sure this book can help you? Possibility thinking moved mountains in my personal life. I know it worked for me. If I communicate the principles to you it will work for you.

Join me now on the most exciting journey of your life as you learn how you too can succeed as a POSSIBILITY THINKER.

II

HOW POSSIBILITY THINKING MOVED MOUNTAINS IN MY LIFE

His car drove past the unpainted barn and stopped in a cloud of summer dust at our front gate. I ran barefooted across the splintery porch and saw my Uncle Henry bound out of the car. He was tall, very handsome, and terribly alive with energy. After many years overseas as a missionary in China, he was visiting our Iowa farm. He ran up to the old gate and put both of his big hands on my four-year-old shoulders. He smiled widely, ruffled my uncombed hair, and said, "Well! I guess you're Robert! I think you are going to be a preacher someday." That night I prayed secretly, "And dear God, make me a preacher when I grow up!" I believe that God made me a POSSIBILITY THINKER then and there.

It was sixteen years later when, after graduation from Hope College in Holland, Michigan, I entered Western Theological Seminary. While a seminary student I was dismayed at the attitude some ambitious students displayed as they prepared to graduate. The great churches of the land loomed as objects to be coveted. "What a dangerous way to go out into the world," I thought. "I can see myself coveting some great church, perhaps scheming to get the job, only to become jealous if someone else is chosen." I didn't want to enter the ministry risking such negative emotions.

About this time I wrote a paper on George Truett, a Baptist minister who in his early years assumed the pastorate of a struggling church in Texas. "I'll give my life . . . the best and all of it, if need be," the young Texan said, "to make this into the greatest church in America!" And he did. When he retired forty years later he left behind the largest, and probably the best, Baptist church in America. What an inspiration! "Give me a chance, God," I prayed, "to build a church from the bottom up. I covet no other man's job. I ask only for an opportunity to create a great job for myself, and

leave behind something wonderful to bless genera-
tions yet unborn."

I was ordained and began my ministry in Ivanhoe,
Illinois, a suburb of Chicago. After four and a half
years a call came to begin a new Protestant church in
Orange County, California. Unfamiliar with the West
Coast, I decided first to visit the area. There I saw
houses springing up from orange groves, the begin-
nings of a tremendous new population explosion but
with few facilities with which to start a new church.
Still undecided, I started back to Chicago. That night
on the train I prayed deeply, asking, "God, should I go
to California?"

It was my moment of decision. It was nearly mid-
night. Wide awake in the top bunk of the Sante Fe
railroad car, I stared out the window. The train was
stopped now, high in the Arizona mountains. A full
moon fell on the snow-covered pines. Suddenly a deer
leaped from behind a tree and bounded off into the
moonlit night spraying dry snow-dust in his trail.
Then, sparked by George Truett's experience, it came
to me: the positive possibility thought,

"The greatest churches have yet to be organized."

That did it. By the grace of God I was being given the
answer to my five-year-old prayer. Here was my
chance to build a great church. My decision was
made. We would accept this challenge and move to
California. We would begin a new church. When I
stepped off the train in Chicago my wife could read
the answer on my face. "I see we're going to California, honey!" she said.

The roads from Illinois to California can be dangerous in February but all went well; the roads were dry
all the way. In Sioux City, Iowa, I parked in front of a

music store. In my pocket was four hundred dollars, a farewell gift from our Chicago congregation. The store's proprietor, my friend Howard Duven, sold me a small electronic organ on the terms I offered: Four hundred dollars down and forty-five dollars a month for thirty-six months; it was to be delivered in California.

It was February 27 when we stopped our old Chevy in front of the tiny house that my sponsoring denomination, the Reformed Church, had arranged as our residence "until you have the money to build a home of your own." Also waiting for me, from the same group, was a check for five hundred dollars.

Wiser people than I considered my denominational affiliation to be a serious disadvantage. For the Reformed Church in America had only 200,000 members in the entire country. My first task upon unpacking in Garden Grove was to find the people living there who belonged to this denomination. I could find only two other families. How could we build a strong following? Obviously the Methodists, Presbyterians, Episcopalians, Baptists, Lutherans, and Catholics would all go to their own churches. Who would come to our church? Reformed people? But there were only two! The odds were that no more than seventy-five families, at the most, could be expected to move into the area in the next ten years! How could we succeed? Looking at some statistics, it was very plain that half the people in the U.S. had no religious affiliation. Our answer then came quickly and clearly. The unchurched thousands —this was our opportunity. We would have to impress and win the people who, for one reason or another, had never before been interested in organized religion.

Three days after we arrived our organ was delivered. I took stock of my assets: a wife, one mortgaged organ, five hundred dollars and the freedom to spend it any way I chose.

All I would have to do was find an empty hall and start preaching. "No, Bob," my advisers from the area informed me. "We looked around before we called you and there is nothing available." NOTHING—what a ghastly impossible word! I refused to accept this negative advice. On my fourth day in California I began searching for a place to hold church services. Surely there must be a place. I started to exercise possibility thinking.

First, I made a list of all the possible places where I might conduct church services. I contacted the school board and learned that California law does not permit a school building to be used for religious purposes. Possibility No. 1 struck out.

I remembered that Seventh-Day Adventists conducted their religious services on Saturday, leaving their buildings empty on Sunday. I was too late. The Presbyterians were worshiping there. Possibility No. 2 struck out.

Next, the mortuary chapel. The Baptists were one step ahead of me. Possibility No. 3 struck out.

Then, on to the Moose Hall. There, again, another denomination had already claimed it. Possibility No. 4 struck out.

I was up to Possibility No. 5. Five years before, my honeymooning wife and I had attended church services in a drive-in theater at Spirit Lake, Iowa. I began looking for a drive-in theater. Three miles east of our new California home I found the Orange Drive-In Theater. The manager listened curiously but politely to my peculiar request. A week later he telephoned, "It's yours to use on Sunday." "Thank you very much. I'll take it," I answered.

Immediately I sensed that this was the beginning of

something new and exciting. I promptly made my first immodest public announcement: "In three weeks we will be starting what will become Orange County's newest and most inspiring Protestant Church." I added, "Come as you are in the family car."

The announcements were precise: "On Sunday, March 27, 1955, at 11:00 A.M., first services will be held in the Orange Drive-In Theater."

It wasn't long before I had some reactions from various community and church leaders. "What? A drive-in church? I never heard of such a thing!"

"I hear you're going to have to begin in a drive-in theater. You poor fellow. How unfortunate that you couldn't find some empty hall," a fellow member of the cloth said.

I was both pitied and criticized as word spread through my staid old denomination that I was going to have to preach from the sticky tar-paper roof of the snack bar of a drive-in theater. "What an undesirable way to begin a church," was the general reaction from the more sympathetic churchmen.

Eight days before our opening service I had an unnerving visit from a friend who was also a Protestant minister. He was the most sincere impossibility thinker I've ever met.

"What's this I hear, Bob? You really aren't planning to start a new church in a drive-in theater, are you?" he asked with a shocked stare. Glaring at me from his judgmental eyes he sermonized, "Why that place is nothing but a passion pit." I reminded him that St. Paul preached on Mars Hill, "and that wasn't such a holy spot." He was unmoved by my simple defense. He promptly proceeded to spend two hours showing me what was wrong with the idea. He left me a priceless illustration of how the impossibility thinker thinks. He warned me that it "couldn't possibly work." He used his impossibility-complexed imagination to dream up all sorts of reasons why my decision was a mistake.

By the time my pious preacher friend with his defeat-prophesying mind left, I found that I had been infected. Impossibility thinking is a highly contagious disease.

That Saturday night I tossed in my bed. My caller had filled my mind with confidence-shattering fear. But what could I do? The announcements were out. I had already spent almost all of the five hundred dollars: twenty-five to buy a homemade trailer to transport the organ to the theater; seventy dollars on a microphone so I could be heard through the theater's public address system; another hundred dollars for lumber with which I had already built a pulpit, altar, and twenty-five-foot cross that I planned to erect on the theater roof. I shuddered with the onslaught of self-doubt. It was three o'clock that Sunday morning before I finally fell asleep.

"Let's go to Hollywood Presbyterian and listen to Ray Lindquist," I suggested to my wife at breakfast. On our way we wondered how many we would have in the drive-in theater the next Sunday. Seated in the pew, at the world's largest Presbyterian church, we opened the bulletin to read the title of the morning message, "God's Formula for Your Self-Confidence." Good! I could certainly use a little self-confidence. The minister began with a text that became the one sentence I would cling to all week, all year, and all through my life: "Being confident in this one thing, that God who has begun a good work in you, will complete it." (Philippians 1:6) Dr. Lindquist assured his audience: "God got you started in life, God has helped you to get where you are, and you can be sure that God will not quit on you."

"God will not quit on you. You may quit on God but God does not quit on you." How these words healed my mind, curing me from the fresh infection of fear. I became a POSSIBILITY THINKER again. Once more I saw the possibility of teaming up with God to work a miracle in Orange County.

The next week I was busily occupied organizing for the Sunday service. On Saturday night I went to the garage and rubbed my hand over the polished mahogany organ. It was firmly bolted to the trailer. I checked the back seat of my car. It was loaded with offering plates, pulpit Bible, microphone, raincoat and umbrella. I checked the air in the trailer tires.

"How many do you think you will have tomorrow morning?" my wife asked as I stepped back in the house.

"Well, we know the choir will be coming from Los Angeles. Nice of that church to loan us their music for a day. There are thirty members in the choir and I've asked them to come in as many cars as possible so the place won't look completely empty." We both laughed. "We should have another ten or twenty cars," I guessed.

"What are you preaching on tomorrow morning?" my wife asked. I recited my text: "If you have faith as a grain of mustard seed you can say to this mountain move, and nothing will be impossible unto you."

That night I woke up once to find myself remembering: "He that has begun a good work in you will complete it." Then I went back to a sound and restful sleep.

The next afternoon my wife and I sat around the dinner table counting the first offering. "About fifty cars. That must mean about twenty families that came from nowhere. Some of them will be back. Thank God it didn't rain. In two weeks it will be Easter. We are on the way, honey!" That enthusiastic report to my wife was strengthened when we finished counting the offering—$83.75. It was a great success.

My impossibility-thinking preacher friend didn't think so. He called the next morning to inquire how we had done. I told him, "Over one hundred people in all." (I didn't tell him that included the visiting choir.) "Is that all?" he lamented, adding, with condescending sympathy, "Well, what can you expect in a drive-in theater." "But that is a hundred per cent increase over last week's attendance," I protested, challenging, "How much of an increase did you have yesterday over the past week?" He admitted his attendance was "down a little for some strange reason he hadn't figured out yet."

I hung up the telephone, returned to my typewriter, and typed a press release: "Southern California's first Drive-In Church got off the ground yesterday with an attendance of over half a hundred cars."

So we were off and away. It was the beginning of something great. We felt it. We knew it. So did the people who were there.

Things moved rapidly for the next few months. With funds borrowed from our denominational headquarters we purchased two acres of land where we hoped to build our church home.

I heard about an excellent architect in Long Beach and went to his office. "I am twenty-eight years old, sir," I said. "I have no money. Will you take a chance and draw plans for a beautiful chapel?" Richard Shelley took a chance even though he knew my salary was only three hundred dollars a month. I signed a contract promising to pay what would amount to a total of over four thousand dollars. When he sent his first bill I simply made an announcement to my small congregation which then contributed enough to meet the payment of one thousand dollars. When final drawings were submitted another offering was collected—three thousand dollars. The plans ready, money was borrowed to build our first chapel. Six months later and after eighteen months of preaching in the open air the chapel was completed. Excitement mounted as the congregation, now numbering two hundred members, prepared to move from the drive-in theater into its beautiful new church home.

It was about this time that I met Rosie Gray.

It began with a telephone call. "You don't know me, Reverend, but my name is Warren Gray. My wife and I have been coming to your church since that first Sunday in the drive-in theater. We live twenty-one miles from the theater. I know it's a long way but could you come to see us?"

When I pulled up to the old rancher's home he was waiting on the front porch for me. He respectfully took off his old felt hat, shook hands, and said, "Before you meet my wife I should tell you that she can't walk and she can't talk. You see, she had a stroke some years ago. She can only grunt a little, and cry a little, and smile faintly. But her mind is good. We never miss church. I'm old but I'm still strong. I just lift her up, put her in the front seat of the car and we drive out and sit there and listen to you talk about faith. It's wonderful. We want to join your church."

I followed Mr. Gray into the house. There was his wife, Rosie, sitting in her chair. Her chin slumped on her chest. Her eyes stared straight out from a head unable to turn. Her mouth hung open. She looked drugged and dazed.

"Hello Rosie, I'm Reverend Schuller."

A faint smile tried to cross her face.

"You want to join the church, Rosie?" I asked.

As her open lips moved slightly, her eyes lifted to

meet mine and tears slid slowly down her cheeks. From the paralyzed lips that struggled vainly to pronounce words she managed a long sustained mumble. The love of God shining from her face told me what she was trying to say.

Two weeks later we baptized Rosie and her husband in their car.

Now we had 202 members.

The following week at a board meeting to plan the grand opening of our beautiful new chapel, someone asked, "What will we do about Rosie Gray?" There were a lot of suggestions. She might listen to religious services on television.

"Why not hold services in our new chapel from nine-thirty until ten-thirty and then Reverend Schuller can go back to the drive-in and conduct a service there from eleven until twelve o'clock for Rosie. There may be others who have a similar need, who would prefer remaining in their cars."

I don't remember who suggested that solution to our problem. The idea carried.

So, eighteen months after arriving in California to organize a new church I found myself with two growing congregations meeting in two separate locations three miles apart!

A year passed. Every Sunday it was the same procedure: A preaching service from nine-thirty to ten-thirty to two hundred people gathered in the chapel. Then a mad dash in my car, pulling a trailer with the organ behind, to the drive-in theater where another two hundred people were waiting for a service to begin at eleven o'clock. Three more years of the same and the dream started evolving in my mind. Why not merge the chapel and the drive-in congregation in one big inspiring creation? After all, when J. Wallace Hamilton of the St. Petersburg Community Church in

Florida found his church too small to hold the growing crowds, he put loudspeakers in the parking area. People worshiped in their cars. People were worshiping both inside and outside at the same time.

Why not find a great architect to *design* a church where people could worship in their cars? There were those unable to walk; those with small children they couldn't leave at home alone; those with emotional problems which made it difficult for them to meet and speak with others; those who labored at manual jobs with no time to change to suitable clothes. For these it was a blessing to be able to remain in their cars to worship. Otherwise they might never get to church. For the others, there would be more conventional pews and accommodations.

The dream began to take clear form in my mind. I could see a sanctuary with glass walls, gardens, fountains leaping in the sunlight, bells hanging in open towers, all rising from acres of tree-shaded grounds. I longed to share my dream with someone, but I did not dare until one day in a church I noticed a calendar that featured this positive sentence:

> **"I would rather attempt to do
> something great and
> fail, than attempt
> to do nothing and succeed!"**

That did it. I began talking with knowledgeable, POSSIBILITY THINKING people, including architects, and became fortified in my conviction that it was a practical and valuable idea. With God's help I was determined to lead this idea to success even if it should take all of my life and all of my energy and my last dime.

Taking the first step, I enthusiastically shared my

dream with the congregation in a sermon entitled
"How to Make Your Dreams Come True." I used the
dream of a walk-in drive-in church as an illustration.
"Perhaps God would love to see a church where people could worship both inside and outside at the same
time. Perhaps God wants us to develop something totally new, to fill a real human need. It can be unsurpassed as a place of peace and beauty."

Now the POSSIBILITY THINKERS in the church would
not let the dream die. "Let's call for a congregational
meeting to discuss the proposal," they said. This was
safe. (No intelligent person can object to a meeting to
discuss a positive proposal.) So the meeting was
called. *We focused our attention on the problem that
needed to be solved.* We faced the facts. Fact number
one: We had two congregations meeting every Sunday
morning in two separate locations. Fact number two:
This drive-in ministry was filling a vital need. Fact
number three: We had church members who needed
the drive-in service. The fourth fact: We had no idea
how long we could continue to use the drive-in theater. We had no lease. We could be told any day that
we would no longer be able to meet there. Fact
number five: It was unpractical for me as pastor to
continue in perpetuity to serve two growing congregations in two separate locations.

We offered the congregation three possible solutions
to these problems:

1. That we divide the two groups into two separate
churches.

2. That we drop the drive-in ministry.

3. That we agree to merge both groups on a new piece
of property in a "walk-in drive-in" church "giving God
a chance to show us how it could be done." We would
simply get out of God's way and give Him a chance to

show us the possible good such a venture could accomplish and the possible ways in which it could be acceptably carried out.

While the congregation debated the three proposals, one POSSIBILITY THINKER, Dr. Wilfred Landrus, was writing on a scrap of paper. After the various alternatives had been honestly debated and a lull fell over the meeting, as so often happens in a problem-busting, tension-generating, brainstorming meeting, Dr. Landrus rose and, reading from his paper, said, "Mr. Chairman, I move that this congregation under God go on record as favoring merger, and that we authorize the consistory to conduct further study toward acquiring property for this purpose." After further debate, the vote was taken. Fifty-five people voted yes, and forty-six voted no. By a slim majority, the decision was made.

The disagreeing congregation went home while I stayed and prayed alone in the dark chapel. As I rose to leave I saw the paper with Dr. Landrus's motion. I picked it up and put it in my pocket. I felt this was an important document in my life and for others.

Thus a great project was begun—an idea, a meeting, and a carried motion.

Opposition immediately mounted. Fortunately, support mounted even faster. A real-estate salesman called me with an offer: "If you are serious about your plan, I know where you can buy ten good acres of land for sixty-six thousand dollars, nineteen thousand down and four hundred a month for fifteen years. If you will put one thousand dollars down now to open a one-hundred-twenty-day escrow you can have it. If in the one-hundred-twenty-day escrow period you do not succeed in coming up with the balance of the down payment or another eighteen thousand dollars, you will, of course, forfeit the thousand dollars with which you have officially accepted the purchase offer." The proposal was placed to the congregation.

There were those who wanted to play it safe. "Let's not agree to buy this land until we have the total nineteen thousand dollars down payment. *Let's not risk losing a thousand dollars.*"

A sharply contrary opinion was offered: "Let's accept the offer tonight. We have eleven hundred dollars in the bank. Let's take one thousand and trust that in the next one hundred nineteen days we can come up with the eighteen thousand to complete the down payment. *Let's not risk losing the opportunity.* If we wait until we have the entire nineteen thousand it may be too late." By a narrow and noisy vote, this second opinion won out. The next morning one thousand dollars was drawn out of our bank. The escrow was opened. We had 119 days left to find eighteen thousand dollars.

Three and one-half months passed. The fund grew to twelve thousand dollars. I was instructed by the church board to close the escrow by depositing the eighteen thousand dollars whenever I had managed to collect the full amount. One hundred fifteen days passed. I cashed in the family's insurance policies. By now I had tapped and exhausted all resources. All we had was fifteen thousand dollars.

It was twelve o'clock noon of the closing day of escrow. In four hours the escrow office would close its doors for the weekend. I was still three thousand dollars short. At twelve o'clock on the final day I could see the opportunity slipping forever away. I went to a telephone booth and called my wife. "Honey, it doesn't look like we are going to make it." "Call Mr. Gray," she said. "But I can't," I argued. Two weeks before, Warren Gray had been sent home from the hospital with an incurable cancer. "Bob, I know that God wants that property. And I know that you should call Mr. Gray," my wife insisted. I hung up the telephone. I prayed quietly. I dialed. My eyes were wet. I wanted to cry. My lips quivered. The ranch phone rang. I conveyed my brief message to the nurse who answered and said, "Just a minute. I think Warren will want to talk to you." A moment later the weak voice of the old sick rancher sounded on the other end of the line. "I've got good news for you, Warren," I pretended. "I can give you the two thousand dollars back that you donated to buy the land. You see, the escrow closes today and we didn't make our goal," I added, trying to be brave. "Oh no, Reverend!" the tired voice objected. "I can do more than I have. I'll meet you in the Bank of America office on North Main Street, Santa Ana, in about an hour. I've got three thousand dollars for you." Dazed, I walked four blocks to the bank office. Warren arrived, went to the cashier's window, and then placed three thousand dollars in my hand, saying, "Reverend, I think God wants that ten acres of ground. And Rosie needs the drive-in church. And after Rosie's gone there will be others like her." He turned around, walked out, and drove twenty miles back to his country home, while I walked down the street to the Orange County Title & Trust Company one hour before the closing of the 120-day time period and placed eighteen thousand dollars on the escrow desk! And that's how God took title to His ten acres.

We had passed many hurdles in our project. Two stormy congregational meetings were now history. One obstacle remained, the sale of our three-year-old stained glass chapel. Sale of property required denominational approval. A meeting of denominational officials was held. Opposing members of the church spoke against "Schuller's plan." They were not without support by a few tradition-bound churchmen who saw only great danger in a drive-in church. But again a motion authorizing us to sell the property was made, supported, and after heated debate the vote was called for. "The ayes have it," the chairman ruled. Before a closing prayer could be offered I saw the five leading members of my church rise and walk out. The next morning I came to my office to find on my desk the minutes of our church board. The secretary of the board was resigning. I also found the financial records. The treasurer was resigning. I found a letter from the vice president—he was quitting too. Suddenly my stomach sank. The three officers of the church were quitting on me. The telephone rang. For some reason my secretary was late. I answered. It was my secretary. "Sorry, Bob, I think the world of you but with this tension I just can't continue to work there now. I'm sorry." And she hung up. I never felt more alone in my life.

Suddenly in this black moment I recalled a Bible verse I had learned as a child: "No man having put his hands to the plough and looking back is fit for the Kingdom of God." I typed these words on paper, slipped them under the glass top of my desk, and read them a dozen times every day. These words gave me *faith with holding power*. And along side of these words, I clipped the words of Dr. Butler of Baylor University: "When things get tough—don't move. People and pressures shift but the soil remains the same no matter where you go." If that wasn't enough I added the old high-school-gymnasium words: "Winners never quit and quitters never win."

However, I could see the church disintegrating, our dreams threatened with disaster. "Tell me, Lord, what you want me to do!" I prayed. "*I will build My church!*"—the words of Jesus Christ came suddenly and clearly into my mind. Until that moment I felt that I was the head of the church. Did I not begin this church? Did I not go out and round up the first five, ten, fifteen, twenty members? Did I not personally make the down payment and the monthly payments on the little organ? And was I not the president of the corporation and the chairman of the board?

Now I realized that Jesus Christ was offering to take over the mountainous responsibilities as head of the church. I may have been over-dramatic but the truth is I stepped out of my chair, stretched out an open hand to my empty seat and said, "Then Lord, You sit there. If You want this walk-in drive-in church to be built, that's wonderful. And if for some reason You don't want this dream to materialize, I'll accept that too. Right now I'll be immensely relieved if You will please take command."

I turned, walked out of His office, and left for a vacation, confident that the dream was now in the hands of Jesus Christ.

Ten days later the impossible mountain started to move. In a wonderful way the problems began to dissolve.

Our chapel was sold at an honest profit. Architectural plans of a beautiful walk-in drive-in church were engineered and approved. We announced the ground-breaking ceremony to herald the beginning of what would be a million-dollar institution specializing in inspiration.

About one hundred cars drove onto our unsightly ten acres to witness the ground-breaking. Long ribbons on stakes marked the outline where the building would stand. Ceremoniously we turned the first spade. The photographers captured the moment. We were on our way. All because of a woman who could not walk or talk.

There was only one touch of sadness. Rosie Gray

had died two days before. The day after God pushed us into our project, Rosie Gray was buried. As I stood with Warren Gray on the wind-swept country cemetery not far from the blue Pacific Ocean, I paraphrased an old saying, with deep feeling: "They also serve who only sit and wait."

Two years later the project was completed. We had successfully borrowed the hundreds of thousands of needed dollars economic experts had told us were financially impossible for such a small congregation to obtain. A four-square-block parcel of ground was graded, paved, and landscaped. Ten miles of wires and another ten miles of pipes, sewers, and electrical conduits crisscrossed under the improved ten acres. A quarter mile of streets, curbs, gutters, water and gas lines had been developed. A great glass cathedral seating one thousand people and a landscaped parking lot equipped with over one hundred hi-fi speakers piping the sound into cars filled with worshiping people—all was finished. Four bell towers, one hundred feet high, holding twelve bells, cut a dramatic silhouette on the skyline. Twelve fountains, reminding us of twelve common men who became the great uncommon leaders of the Christian religion, leaped out of a block-long reflection pool that adorned the 250-foot-long east wall of the sanctuary. Now that the work was finished, would it be a success? On Sunday morning, November 5, 1961, Norman Vincent Peale flew from New York to preach the first sermon from the pulpit of this church —unlike any church ever before built in the history of religion. He mounted the pulpit and looked across a drive-in parking area filled with five hundred cars carrying nearly two thousand worshipers. He looked across the upholstered pews of the sanctuary crowded with over one thousand people. The choir sang "Holy, Holy, Holy." I pressed a button—and two twenty-five-foot-high sections of the glass wall alongside the pulpit separated slowly like angel's wings opening. Now the minister in the pulpit could look clearly out at both the walk-in and drive-in worshipers. It worked. Beautifully. Over four thousand people that were there were sure—this was a success. A handful of POSSIBILITY THINKERS had tested and proved the reality of POSSIBILITY THINKING. Today a staff of five ministers serves six thousand people weekly in this church. Our property has a valuation of over one and a half million dollars, and more construction is planned.

What does it all prove? That it is possible to achieve seemingly impossible goals by possibility thinking. That a seemingly helpless person like Rosie Gray may be used by God for very important purposes.

It proves that God keeps His promises. "He that has begun a good work in you will complete it."

What does it say to you? I hope it says that you too can make your dreams come true.

If you have faith as a grain of mustard seed you can say to this mountain move—and nothing shall be impossible unto you.

What would you like to build? A church? Probably not. A business? A career? A home? A marriage? A great reputation? A life that will really amount to something?

Then you can!

The first step is to get rid of that impossibility complex.

III

AN EIGHT-STEP TREATMENT
FOR THAT
IMPOSSIBILITY COMPLEX

You know now that there are two kinds of people in the world: *Possibility Thinkers* and *Impossibility Thinkers*. Which are you?

To find out, take this test. Answer honestly as you ask yourself these questions:

1. Do I look for reasons why something can't be done instead of searching for ways in which it can be done?

2. Do I ever make decisions out of fear?

3. Do I tend to resist new ideas and prefer to do things the way I've always done them?

4. Do I move ahead only when I have every single fact?

5. Do I have a tendency to demand a guarantee of success before I begin?

6. Do I imagine the opposition I will encounter without imagining the support I might expect?

7. Do I ever turn down an idea simply because I don't like it or because my mind is already made up or because I've made other plans?

8. Do I ever close my mind to a suggestion before hearing the full explanation?

9. Do I point out the disadvantages in an idea before I point out the advantages?

10. Do I ever make negative decisions because I am tired and it's easier?

11. If I can't imagine a solution to a problem am I inclined to turn away from it?

12. Do I believe that human nature can't really be altered; that a man's life can't be changed?

If you have answered many of these questions in the affirmative then the chances are very good that you are suffering from an impossibility complex.

However, you can overcome that impossibility complex. You can become a possibility thinker if you want to become one.

**Great discipline
generates enormous strength.**

Can we break deeply ingrained negative thought habits? Emphatically yes! If a dog can be trained to discipline, so can a human being. This is one of the truths that Pavlovian psychology has made very clear. The Russian psychologist Pavlov proved in his dog experiments that it is possible to completely reorient the thought processes of a human being. So he "invented" a procedure which is at the basis of what is popularly called "brainwashing." It has been used negatively by Communists. But it can be used as a positive, constructive, healing, life-transforming procedure. Constantly feeding the brain positive thoughts will eventually transform the thinking procedure.

THE IMPOSSIBILITY THINKER
CAN BECOME
A POSSIBILITY THINKER

Now try this eight-step treatment for the impossibility complex.

It will not be enough to simply read this chapter. You may have to reread the parts which apply to you, or are most important to you, over and over again. *Read it out loud.*

If you really believe these eight points
if you really follow each point religiously,
your life will change. The world around you
will change. For you will have changed your
thinking. TRANSFORMED THINKING transforms
everything.

1. *REMOVE YOUR DISADVANTAGE COMPLEX.*

Build strong self-confidence and you are on your way. You do this by attacking the disadvantage complex. Don't be tricked, tripped, and trapped by these disadvantage complexes if one or more are bothering you.

"I'm too old"

The truth is, you are never too old to change. You are not too old to change until you give up. Only when you reach a point where you don't care any more—then, and only then—are you old. You are not old until you have lost your vision. That's why thousands of octogenarians have astonished the world with the sudden discovery of talents that lay buried deep within them for over eighty years before they were discovered. Grandma Moses is only one example.

"I'm handicapped"

The most serious handicap any person can have is an impossibility complex (and you are breaking that right now). My wife has a cousin named Frank Vander Maaten. At the age of eighteen he was one of the most accomplished violinists in Sioux County, Iowa. Then a terrible accident happened in his father's blacksmith shop. A red hot iron fell on his left hand. The four fingers that touched the strings of his violin were cut off! Only his thumb remained on his mutilated hand. Handicapped? Not in his thinking! He determined to learn to play the violin left-handed. And he did, holding the bow in his mutilated hand. He became a prominent violinist in the Sioux City, Iowa, Symphony.

A blind person once said: "I thought when I lost my sight I would be doomed to unhappiness. Now I have discovered that I am happier without my sight. Most of my unhappy thoughts came in through my eyes—I saw new styles and became dissatisfied with what I had. I saw handsome faces of other people and was dissatisfied with my own looks. Most joy-producing thoughts come into people's minds in the dark anyway. Don't you close your eyes when you kiss the one you love? Don't you close your eyes when you listen to good music? Don't you close your eyes when you pray?" This blind person has learned to paint without eyesight. You are not handicapped until you think you are.

"I don't have the time, money, or energy to do what I'd like to do"

Are you sure? Read the chapters in this book on

time, money, and energy. Read them with an open mind before you accept and believe this impossibility thought.

"I am from a lowly background"

So what? No one's background or past is a disadvantage unless he makes it so in his thinking! Remember, any disadvantage rightly handled can be turned into an advantage. A young man with a hillbilly background could have allowed himself to develop an inferiority complex when he came to the big city. But he was honest, friendly, natural, warm, and instead of letting his "disadvantage" work against him, he turned it to his advantage. I am thinking of Tennessee Ernie Ford.

"I came from a broken home. I had an awful childhood."

"My parents quarreled, then divorced, and I was shuttled back and forth. I am afraid I am an emotional cripple for the rest of my life." Is that so? Only if you want it to be so. I am thinking of a child who was born of a prostitute mother. The ill-famed mother abandoned her baby on the doorstep of the father's home only to be cast out on the streets by the jealous wife of the child's father. The youngster grew up in the slums —poor, rejected, unloved, abandoned. What happened? This lad met Jesus Christ! Christ came into that boy's life. And he grew up to be the greatest Japanese minister and poet of the twentieth century. His name, Kagawa, is an inspiration to millions.

"I don't know the right people"

So what? Get acquainted with big people, if you have a reason. Don't be afraid. Successful and important people are usually interested in helping other people with good ideas. All you need is the nerve to write a letter, place a long-distance telephone call, send a telegram, and you will be in touch with great people who are always looking for new friends and projects to enrich their lives. The really great people are interested in creative and constructive ideas. Perhaps the most famous minister in the world at the time I was beginning our church was Norman Vincent Peale. I wrote him a letter and was amazed to receive an immediate reply. We have become wonderful friends. He has been immensely helpful. When I needed a great architect I tried for the man who I felt was the world's greatest—Richard Neutra. I was astonished when I easily reached him on a long-distance line. We have become wonderful friends. You can build a friendship with famous people if you forget your inferiority feelings, muster great nerve, and walk up confidently to enthusiastically introduce yourself.

"My skin is not the right color"

"I can never really do what I want to do because of my race." Is that so? What do you want to do? What do you want to be? You can do, or be, almost anything you can dream or desire. POSSIBILITY THINKING is the greatest weapon that a person who feels inferior because of race or nationality can acquire. Once POSSIBILITY THINKING is acquired, then the imagination is no longer tyrannized, tripped, or tricked by IMPOSSIBILITY THINKING. There are so many illustra-

tions of the truth of this by so many members of
POSSIBILITY-THINKING minority groups in America that
one does not know where to begin. Robert Weaver,
the first American Negro to hold cabinet office, had
this idea drummed into him as a child by his mother:
"The way to offset color prejudice is to be awfully
good at whatever you do."

"I don't have a good education"

"My I.Q. is lower than others." So what. "First
prizes don't always go to the brightest and strongest
man. Again and again, the man who wins is the man
who is sure that he can." I was told once by a man
who knows. His college entrance test was disappoint-
ingly low. Nevertheless he was admitted through influence. He developed a terribly low estimate of himself. As a result he never really tried. He was sure that
he was a C student, and that is just what he turned out
to be. Of course he was getting exactly what he was
going after! Unfortunately, the admission tests did not
measure the qualities that really make the difference
between success and failure. They did not measure
"imagination," "determination," "integrity," "sincerity,"
"intuitive gifts of diplomacy," etc. Had a psychological
test been devised and given at that time to that student on these all-important character traits, he would
have been rated much higher. He would have acquired a far better academic record. As it all worked
out, this man's real gifts became apparent, not in his
IMPOSSIBILITY THINKING academic world, but out in
the hard-hitting world where his enterprising and resourceful spirit and his POSSIBILITY THINKING attitude
have made him one of the most successful men in his
chosen profession. He refused to allow his "intellectual

disadvantages" to keep him from being a dignified success.

2. DEVELOP THE HABIT OF RECOGNIZING AND RESPONDING TO THE SMALLEST TRICKLE OF POSITIVISM THAT MIGHT LEAK INTO YOUR MIND. One small possibility thought can overpower many impossibility thoughts, if the possibility thought is given a chance to survive and thrive. During the Second World War England had blackouts. When enemy bombers were sighted all lights in the city were extinguished. It was learned that the smallest lighted candle could be seen from miles in the air. Don't measure power by size. One powerful possibility thought, allowed to remain in the brain, has enormous life-changing power. Harbor and feed a possibility thought and in an astonishingly short time the mind will be overtaken by the power of hope which all began with one trickle of possibility thinking.

"I don't believe in God any more. There is no God. I thought so once. But He left me. And I am in hell now. And I know there is no God." She was a very sick woman. Visiting her in a mental hospital, I failed to plant a single seed of faith in her totally darkened mind. Some time later I returned and found her absolutely transformed. What had happened? A young doctor walking through the ward had casually stopped to chat with her. He found no response from this terribly lost soul. "What's your name?" he asked. She didn't answer. "Well, my name is Dr. Heven," he said. Slowly she raised her head. Her hollow eyes stared at this white-coated man in front of her. The doctor prepared to leave when she touched his sleeve. He stopped. She looked hungrily up to him and uttered her first words. "What's your name?" He smiled and said, "Dr. Heven." She dropped her head, and he walked on. But into her mind leaked this thought: "Dr. Heven. Heven. If Heven is here then this can't be hell. If Heven is here God must be here. God is here." And even though this thinking was irrational, it was the beginning of the birth of hope.

The next morning she walked down the corridor repeating out loud a Bible verse which she had often heard. It was returning from the sunken depths of her memory, and she was repeating it now quite unconsciously: "This is the day which the Lord has made. Let us rejoice and be glad in it." She kept repeating this phrase through the day. The next morning she repeated it again—now with a smile—like a person slowly awakening from a deep and terrible nightmarish sleep. "This is the day which the Lord has made. I will rejoice and be glad in it." Now the healing power of this powerful Bible verse was doing its good work. She had forgotten about "Dr. Heven," and her returning reason automatically rejected this irrational "heaven-is-here-therefore-God-is-here thinking." Her health improved. She began responding to treatment. When I saw her I was awe-struck at the fantastic transformation. Today, three years later, she is fully recovered and teaching school.

3. *BEGIN EACH DAY WITH A POSITIVE SEED THOUGHT AND HOLD IT THERE.* Dress your mind when you dress your body. No discreet person would go into the world half dressed. No wise person will consider himself well dressed unless his mind is wearing a "positive idea" as a shield against the negative forces that will strike him before his workday begins. Make a hobby of collecting "shields for the spirit" that can fortify your mind as you move into the workaday world. Try these spirit shields:

Luke 1:37   "With God nothing shall be impossible."

Mark 10:27   "With men it is impossible, but not with God."

Matthew 19:26   "But with God all things are possible."

Mark 10:27   "For with God all things are possible."

Luke 18:27   "The things which are impossible with men are possible with God."

Mark 9:23   "If you can believe all things are possible to him who believes."

Mark 14:36   "Father, all things are possible."

Matthew 17:20   "If you have faith as a grain of mustard seed you can say to this mountain move, and nothing shall be impossible."

Our family eats breakfast together. Before we scatter our separate ways, we have our "spiritual vitamin" for the day. It is always a short Bible verse—short enough to memorize easily so we can hold it before our minds all day. I, in my office, in bumper-to-bumper traffic, in my calling, and in counseling; my wife, at home, in shopping, and in answering the telephone; my children in school and in the playground. No man is dressed to go out until he has dressed his mind with a fresh, clean, comfortable-fitting, protective idea.

4. *EXPOSE THE BRAIN TO A CONSTANT POSITIVE DIET*. If you want something worthwhile to come out of your mind, you have to put something worthwhile into it. Cultivate the discriminatory art.

Does this television program, this literature, this conversation, inspire me? Or does it depress me? Does it help me want to be a better person, or is it neutral and unstimulating? Does it evoke the positive emotions of love, faith, hope, and joy, or the negative emotions of hate, disbelief, fear, and misery? Am I feeding my mind a diet that will calm, challenge, uplift, or inject determination to go out and win?

Stop listening to those impossibility thinkers who tell you how wrong you are—how impossible your idea is.

As much as possible discipline yourself to an exposure to positivism. Go to the library and find books that will teach you more on the art of becoming a POSSIBILITY THINKER. There are many.

5. GIVE YOURSELF AN "IN-DEPTH" POSSIBILITY-THINKING TREATMENT ONCE A WEEK.

A friend of mine who has had problems with dandruff said, "Every Saturday night, without fail, I have to give myself a good shampoo with a special dandruff-fighting solution. This keeps my problem under control just for one week."

Well, once a week we should give ourselves a spiritual and mental-dandruff-removing treatment. Skip a week and you will feel the difference. Skip two weeks and others will tell the difference.

God knew what He was doing when He ordered the ancient Jews to reserve one day in seven for rest and worship. The rising tide of emotional problems in our country has escalated with the simultaneous rise in a breakdown of the practice of setting one day aside for quietness, rest, and the refreshment of the spirit. Find a place of religious worship that specializes in positive inspiration, and attend weekly. The human being's inspiration tank needs to be refilled every seven days.

That's the way God designed us. Often it's when you don't feel like going to church that you need it most. Your lack of desire for worship is a sure sign that you need inspiration, just as the unenthusiastic sputtering of a slowing car is a certain sign that it is running out of gas.

6. *TALK YOURSELF INTO POSSIBILITY THINKING.* Affirm "I can do all things through Christ who is strengthening me." You can talk yourself into almost any attitude.

Most of us have too often talked ourselves into fatigue, failure, and defeat. Repeat out loud, "I'm tired," "I'm finished," "I'm through"—and you will soon believe it.

The positive application is equally powerful. Repeat out loud, "I'm going to be happy today, though the skies are cloudy and gray, no matter what comes my way, I'm going to be happy today." "I am happy." "I really am happy." "I don't realize I'm happy because I am subconsciously worrying about what is going to happen today or tomorrow. Years from now I will look back on this moment and realize that I was really very happy." As the French author Colette viewed her life story on the screen, someone said, "It looked like you were a very happy child," and she answered, "Yes, it's too bad I didn't realize it at the time."

You are happy. But you may have to tell yourself many times before you realize it. Because you do not feel it you will think the whole idea is perfectly silly. Ridiculous. Furthermore, it sounds dishonest. Your sense of honesty will tend to restrain you from saying it. Don't hold back. Talk yourself into joy, faith, hope, love, happiness, and high achievement.

"It really works. I can't believe it, but it really works. The past four days have been the happiest days

I've had in years. And if it works for a few days, why not for a lifetime?" The man who wrote me that had been in my office only a week before, determined to quit his job of nineteen years. He had complained, "I hate my work. I can't stand it. I never have really liked it. I am only one year from drawing a pension, but I stiffen up every morning at the thought of going to work. I hate it." "Why do you hate it?" I asked. "Let's see your hands—bleeding? No. Is there great danger of being killed on the job? Why do you hate it?" We listed all of the advantages. Now, I demanded, "You have surrendered your will to the thought that you don't like your work. You have allowed your mood to take the form of ideas—you have turned these ideas into words—you've heard yourself declare these words. You believe what you have heard yourself say. You have hypnotized yourself into hating your work. Use the same mental process on the positive side. Repeat, 'I like my work.' " He sat there and just laughed at me. "That's stupid," he said. "I can't say that. I just can't." *"Yes you can, if you want to."* I raised my voice, intentionally loud, to crack the icy surface of his frozen faith. Then I forced him to repeat these words: "I like my work." I made him spend a half hour repeating positive affirmations in my office until he began to get used to the shock of hearing himself talk positively. A week later he wrote, "I really felt stupid when I first started it. But it works. And if it works, why knock it? It has even changed the attitude of my family."

"I don't believe in God. I don't love my husband. And I am going to commit suicide." She sat in my office and blurted out those impossibility statements. Each time she vocalized these impossibility feelings she heard herself talking and she believed herself!

"Become a sanctified liar," I suggested. "You will

think you are lying. But you are not lying. You are really exercising extreme faith. You are saying that you have IT before IT has even arrived. That's real faith. The truth is you believe in God more than you think you do. You love your husband more than you think you do. Repeat after me, even though you think you are lying, these affirmations: 'I love my husband.' 'I love life.' 'I believe in God.'" I spent one hour convincing her to repeat these affirmations. "Always tell yourself the opposite of what you feel—when your feelings are negative," I urged. That was three years ago. She follows this practice faithfully, and has found a rich love for her husband and a vibrant faith in God and a healthy love for life.

IT WILL WORK FOR YOU TOO, IF YOU HAVE THE STRENGTH TO FORCE YOURSELF TO DO IT. *Repeat the following sentences* OUT LOUD. *This will be one of the hardest assignments in this book.* You will feel like a hypocrite, a braggart, and a liar. But read—OUT LOUD—then repeat again and again—LOUDER—these powerful affirmations:

> *I can do great things.*
> *I have great possibilities deep inside me.*
> *I have possibilities that haven't been born yet.*
> *I'm really a wonderful person when Christ lives in me.*
> *I've been too self-critical.*
> *I've been my own worst enemy.*
> *I'm a child of God. God loves me.*
> *I can do all things through Christ who strengthens me.*

Your biggest problem will be to believe it deeply enough to try it long enough and loud enough to dehypnotize yourself from the mesmerizing power of your impossibility thinking.

7. USE PRAYER POWER. Try the prayer that Dr. Daniel Poling says three times every morning, as soon as he arises: "I believe. I believe. I believe!" This kind of prayer really flushes the negative out of the brain! Now repeat: "I can. I can. I can."

Prayer power really works! There is a Higher Power that can and will penetrate the depths of your being to recondition your thought processes. Ask God to help you to become a POSSIBILITY THINKER. Ask Him once, and never again. For if you have sent Him one petition you may be sure He has your message. Stop asking, but don't stop praying. Stop begging and start thanking. To continue to plead will only indicate your lack of faith in His hearing or helping power. To continue to ask will only generate or intensify your emotional misery. This will weaken you. It will not inspire you. It will not strengthen you. Pleading, negative praying only exercises and strengthens your anxieties. Someone said:

> God weighs our prayers,
> he doesn't count them.

In the right way, in the right time, God will answer. So make your prayers affirmative, not negative. Thank Him for hearing your prayer. Thank Him for what He is doing about it. Try this prayer. Repeat it out loud. "Thank you, God, for making me a possibility thinker. Thank you for reminding me that all things are possible if I will dare to believe." This is power-generating, hope-building, anxiety-relieving prayer. Pray yourself up. Don't pray yourself down. Affirmative prayer really works miracles. This was the way Christ prayed: "Abba Father, all things are possible unto you." And when a human being asks God to save him from his

IMPOSSIBILITY COMPLEX, God will help. After all, God wants to see His sons and daughters walk with shoulders back, heads erect, with dignity shining in their faces.

8. HAVE A THOROUGH PERSONALITY CHECK-UP.

Begin with a physical checkup. One morning, a prominent elder walked into a Chicago minister's office and declared, "I just don't believe in God any more." The wise pastor remained calm. Exceptionally perceptive, he suspected that such a radical change in thinking was triggered by some abnormal force. His probing questions led him to suspect that this man was physically ill. He arranged an examination with a medical doctor, who discovered a thyroid deficiency. Medical relief restored spiritual faith. Amazing? Not really. But revealing. So, have a regular physical checkup at least once a year.

An impossibility thinker may also be emotionally sick. Joshua Loth Liebman in his book *Peace of Mind* tells the case history of a very brilliant person who claimed to be an atheist. Depth analysis brought startling information to light. When this brilliant atheist was a little boy he was brought to the synagogue where he was told that God was his Heavenly Father. However, this child's real father was cruel. So the lad's brain defensively rejected the concept of another "Father." He didn't want God. He didn't want another father. Fathers were mean. At that tender age a wounded child's mind set up an emotional roadblock to faith. From that moment on he did not want to believe in God. When this long-forgotten experience was brought to light, this intelligent person realized that his deep-seated doubt had its taproot in a distorted emotional experience. He went on to develop a healthy belief. If you or your family suspects you are emotionally disturbed, check it out with a good doctor.

Then have a good spiritual checkup. How healthy is your religion? Wholesome religion builds up a person's sense of self-dignity. Your self-image will determine to a great degree whether you will be a POSSIBILITY or an IMPOSSIBILITY THINKER. The Jewish religion has always sought to give man a great sense of self-worth. Jesus Christ was inspired by the ancient Jewish faith which taught that man was made in the image of God. The Hebrews believed that the first human was a marvelous creature. Then something terrible happened, and man lost ground emotionally. He lost faith in himself, in God, and in his fellows. Somehow God had to restore man's lost glory. You restore man's glory when you restore his self-image. When he walks straight, clean, upright, with marvelous self-confidence, he is glorifying his God.

Healthy Christianity sets men free from the guilts, fears, worries, and anxieties that would feed feelings of indignity. Real Christianity tells us that we can really be somebody. "You are the salt of the earth. . . . You are the light of the world," Jesus said to his followers. It was said of the early followers of Jesus Christ that "to those who believed Him, to them gave He power to become sons of God." Jesus Christ gives to His followers freedom from oppressive guilt. They know that God is their Father now. That makes them sons of God. Suddenly their sense of self-dignity is restored. They no longer dislike themselves. Here's how Jesus Christ gives a person the sense of self-worth that is an absolute prerequisite to POSSIBILITY THINKING! For if you know that you and God are good friends, then you can go out and say courageously, "If God be for us, who can be against us?" Meet a great POSSIBILITY THINKER and see what you can become.

There were some tough, crude, unschooled fishermen who ran into a fellow years ago. He put his hand on their shoulders and said, "Follow me and I will make you fishers of men!" It was their moment of inspiration. When they were discouraged and felt they didn't amount to anything, He said ,"You are the salt of the earth. . . . You are the light of the world." More than anything they knew that they could be persons in a world of nonpersons. That great inspirer was a wonderful Jew who lived two thousand years ago. His name was Jesus Christ. What a great POSSIBILITY THINKER! Draw close to Him. Catch his spirit and you will never be the same again. Let Jesus Christ redesign your self-image.

Tomorrow morning try this prayer by Norman Grubb:

> Good morning, Christ.
> I love you!
> What are you up to today?
> I want to be part of it!
> Thank you, God.
> Amen!

NOW LET YOUR IMAGINATION PULL THOSE GREAT POSSIBILITIES OUT OF YOU.

IV

LET YOUR IMAGINATION
RELEASE YOUR IMPRISONED
POSSIBILITIES

A polio victim who required an iron lung to breathe learned to breathe without it—even though every muscle below his Adam's apple is paralyzed. Karl Dewayne Sudekum has learned to breathe like a frog.

In 1953 while Karl was a lieutenant in the U. S. Navy, he contracted polio. For six years he could breathe only in an iron lung or on a tilt bed. Then he got mad—really angry. He decided he *would* breathe. He stopped the rocking motion of his tilt bed and remembered how he used to breathe like a frog as a young boy in Nashville, Tennessee. It was a trick almost all the kids knew. He would take air with his tongue and force it down his windpipe. When he exhaled, his lungs let out the air like a deflating balloon. He's been breathing this way ever since.

"Science doesn't really know how it's done," he said. "It's a two-cycle pumping action that some people can do and some can't. Some people can whistle through their teeth, but I never could. It's like that."

He could stay away from the iron lung as long as he remained awake. With his first real independence, Sudekum decided to become an attorney.

In 1959, he entered the University of San Diego. His wife, Emerald, drove him to school and wheeled him into class. He couldn't take notes, and a tape recorder was too awkward. He simply listened and remembered.

Then he was told he had diabetes. That under control, the doctors discovered an ulcer. For a year he lived with a mysterious high fever, a reaction to medication. Still, he got his diploma and passed the bar examination.

He is practicing law now and signs documents K. D. Sudekum. It is too much of a task to write his full name with a pen in his teeth.

When he talks too long in court, his face gets very red, but it's nothing to worry about. A cold is something else. It could be fatal. So what does he do?

"I don't get colds."

If he falls asleep or faints while out on his own, frog-breathing, he will die unless someone who knows his condition administers artificial respiration. What does he do about that?

"I try to think about it as little as possible."

Use your Christ-inspired imagination to think of ways in which you can harness your handicap, profit from your problem, capitalize on your crisis, and perhaps even make your sorrow serve you.

USE YOUR IMAGINATION TO BECOME A SUCCESS IN THE ART OF GETTING ALONG WITH PEOPLE

To succeed in the field of human relations, polish your own personality with your imagination. Visualize yourself as a relaxed, charming, confident, poised, smiling person. Firmly hold this mental image of yourself and you will become this kind of person. The opposite is also true. If you dare to allow your mind to picture yourself "telling people off," "blowing your top," or being irritable, sensitive, and touchy, that is precisely the way you will react, and, I might add, you will fail miserably in the school of human relations. This is the exciting truth: Your imagination has the power to transform and recreate your personality.

More exciting news! You can actually change the personalities of other people through the power of your own imagination. I sat in on a board of directors meeting recently. When I entered the room, I was greeted by the cold, unfriendly stares of six men. *Personalities, like feelings, are terribly contagious.* Because I carelessly neglected to use my sanctified imagination, I naturally allowed myself to "take on" the same frigid, formal, unfriendly front. Then a wonderful thing happened. A strong, friendly personality entered the room. He radiated warmth as his face beamed steadily. His infectious smile refused to fade before the icy stares of these important men. To my amazement within five minutes the personalities of the other people in the room were transformed. Soon we were talking and joking, and sincerely enjoying each other's company. After the meeting, I asked my friend *how he managed to change these stuffed shirts into wonderful people*. His secret was simple. "I paused before I entered that room and imagined myself as a strong, dominant, friendly, down-to-earth person. I imagined the men on the other side of the door as good fellows. I visualized them returning my smiles, and reflecting the kindness I was radiating toward them." This man had discovered how to use his imagination to change the personalities of people.

USE YOUR IMAGINATION
TO MEET NEW PEOPLE

Do you have a problem meeting people? Is it hard for you to make new friends and acquaintances? Then use, with great success, the power of your imagination. I discovered this technique in starting our church. Because I had no members, I decided to go down the street and ring doorbells, telling my story to people face to face. Frankly, I trembled at the thought of going from door to door, meeting all these new people. I imagined being rudely rebuffed every time I rang a doorbell. Generally, we get what we expect. I would walk timidly up to the front door, secretly hoping no one would be at home. More than once I left without ringing the bell. I simply got "cold feet" and went back to my car. Suddenly, in answer to my prayer for divine help and guidance, God sparked my imagination. I began to visualize warm wonderful people on the other side of the doors—people who were eager to meet a new minister. That did it! I approached every door thereafter with this belief: "Behind that door is someone who is going to become a lifelong friend of mine. I am about to make the acquaintance of a man who will become one of my most loyal friends." Try this technique with a problem person. Imagine him as a really fine person at heart. That's exactly what he will become.

USE YOUR IMAGINATION
TO
CATCH A VISION
OF
THE PERSON YOU WERE MEANT TO BE

In his book *The Heart of a Champion*, Bob Richards tells the story of Olympic champion Charley Paddock, who was a great speaker and loved to talk to young people in high school. Once while speaking at East Tech High School in Cleveland, Ohio, he challenged, "If you think you can, you can. If you believe a thing strongly enough, it can come to pass in your life!" Afterward he lifted his hand and said, "Who knows but there's an Olympic champion here in this auditorium this afternoon!" Afterward a spindly-legged Negro boy said to Mr. Paddock, "Gee, Mr. Paddock, I'd give anything if I could be an Olympic champion just like you!" It was that lad's moment of inspiration. From that moment on, his life was changed. In 1936 that spindly-legged boy went to Berlin, Germany. He won four gold medals. His name is Jesse Owens. Back home he was driven through the streets of Cleveland to the cheers of the crowd. The car stopped and he signed some autographs. A little skinny Negro boy pressing against the car said, "Gee, Mr. Owens, I'd give anything if I could be an Olympic champion just like you." Jesse reached out to this little fellow, who was nicknamed "Bones," and said, "You know, young fellow, that's what I wanted to be when I was a little older than you are. If you'll work, and train and believe, then you can become an Olympic champion!" Well, that little fellow was so inspired he ran all the way home. Bob Richards writes, "That little fellow told me that when he got home he ran up to his grandmother and said, 'Grandma, I'm going to become an Olympic champion!' " At Wembley Stadium in London, England, in 1948, six boys waited for the gun to go off for the finals of the 100-meter dash. The gun cracked. The boy in the outside lane burst out, drove down to hit the tape, and won. His name: Harrison "Bones" Dillard. He tied Jesse Owens' Olympic record. And went on to break more world records.

"You say it's fantastic?" Richards asks. "You're saying that it'll never happen again? And I tell you you're wrong. It'll happen again and again, in boys and girls who are inspired. Who will catch a vision of what they can become, who will see not skinny legs or spindly legs, but who will catch a vision of Olympic champions." They will rise through training and perseverance and hard work and they will be champions.

As you face life, throw your shoulders back, look into the sun, and thank God you're a man. When God made you, He gave you what was given to no other living organism in the universe—the immeasurable power to visualize great dreams! This stupendous truth has never been more forcefully, exquisitely phrased than in these inspiring lines: "What is man that Thou are mindful of him and the son of man that Thou visitest him, for Thou has made him a little lower than God." (Psalms 8:4–5) The daring power of human imagination is exciting proof that you are made in the image of God. What an imagination God has displayed! His infinite mind visualized a universe so grandiose in scale, so immense in distance, so far-reaching in miles that no human being will ever be able to see it all in a single lifetime.

Now, the exciting news is that the Creator of Life has shared with the human race His creative power of imagination.

This imagination is latent in your mind this very moment—and it has the power to make you. "As a man thinketh in his heart so is he."

USE YOUR IMAGINATION
TO BECOME
WHAT YOU REALLY WANT TO BE

Use your God-sparked imagination to gain self-confidence. Imagine yourself as inferior, inadequate, mediocre, and that's all you will ever be. Imagine yourself as top notch, successful, a man who is getting ahead, and you will move forward.

I recently heard about William E. Constable, who worked in a lime quarry in Indiana for nine years. One day he came to the conclusion that "my life was a waste, so I decided to get busy and do something with it." That night he came home from the quarry and announced to his wife that he was going to become a lawyer. He resumed his education and finally enrolled in Indiana University. He continued to work in the quarry eight hours a day while he went to school. "My wife and three kids really helped," he adds gratefully. He graduated from Indiana University in 1966 and guess what. He was elected to Phi Beta Kappa! His grade average was 3.95 out of a possible four points. He has gone on to law school. How did he do it? How did he work eight hours a day and come out on top of his college class? Besides crediting the company that employed him and praising his family's cooperation, he offered this insight: "You can do a lot of studying in thirty minutes if you have to." To sum it up, there came that moment when he imagined himself being an attorney and said, "Just because I've spent nine years in a quarry is no reason I can't be a lawyer."

When my daughter was fourteen I began trying to make a possibility thinker out of her. She said, "Daddy, I find this hard to believe. For instance, I'd love to play the violin. But I wouldn't care to be just one of the ten violinists in our high-school orchestra. I would like to be in the first chair."

"Well, why not?" I challenged, half-joking. She took me seriously and announced she was going to study the instrument. She took private lessons. She made the orchestra. She was in tenth chair. She worked harder. The top four chairs were held by students who had been studying privately for many years. Then one day she came home from "the challenges" and proudly announced that she had passed everyone and made first chair. "It really works, Daddy, this possibility thinking really works."

Imagination can transform your physical appearance. Imagine yourself with twinkling eyes, a beaming face, a radiant personality; hold that picture in your mind and you will become that kind of person. Think of yourself as ugly, unattractive, and your eyes will take on a dullness, your facial muscles will droop and a gloomy appearance will suddenly make you unattractive indeed.

Beauty is mind-deep. You are as pretty—or as ugly —as you think you are. Visualize yourself as a pleasant, friendly, cheerful, laughing, sparkling person and your imagination will make you into that kind of person. Now exercise this positive imagination daily and the "smile muscles" will become so strong that your facial appearance will actually be transformed. Through the power of imagination I actually trimmed forty pounds of unsightly fat from my body. I drew a mental image of the kind of physique I wanted and held that vision before me constantly. I also directed the negative power of my imagination toward positive ends in this way: when I saw a luscious piece of banana cream pie, I pictured in my mind a vision of a fat, sloppy, undisciplined man. It's amazing how your imagination can affect the appeal of food! Focus clearly on the screen of your mind the image of the kind of person you want to be and let your God-sparked imagination work its miracles.

It's easy to understand how the imagination operates. When you draw a clear mental picture and get a sharp mental definition of what you really want, then you become enthusiastic about it. Enthusiasm produces ambition. And with the fresh spurt of ambition you begin to pray, plan, and plug; and before you know it your project is off the ground.

What is the secret power of the POSSIBILITY THINKERS? It is their faith. And what is this faith? It is the power of God working through their God-sparked imagination.

Harness the sacramental power of a sanctified imagination.

Truly a sanctified imagination has sacramental power. Religion defines sacrament as a sacred channel through which God performs His great miracles. LET GOD DO SOMETHING NOW—Let Him spark His great ideas into your imaginating mind! Unchain your imagination. Let this God-given power within you go free!

HOW TO MAKE SUCCESS-GENERATING IMAGINATION WORK FOR YOU

1. *PICK A GOAL.* Possibility thinkers are people who believe in setting goals for personal achievement. Almost without exception these goals appear, at first inception, to be unrealistic. But the POSSIBILITY THINKER intuitively knows that nothing is impossible until he stops setting goals.

Make up your mind that goal-setting is absolutely necessary!

"But goal-setting creates great tensions and anxiety," a psychologist said recently in my hearing. He continued, "A major cause of frustration and anxiety in our age is the terrible habit of setting high goals and pressuring ourselves relentlessly." Well, this psychologist had an extreme Freudian attitude towards goals. To Sigmund Freud, the greatest drive in the human breast is the will to pleasure. According to this school of thought, the most important thing in life is tensionless peace of mind. Tension and anxiety then are the modern devils that rob us of our happiness. So goals are dangerous because goals generate tensions! By contrast the great psychiatrist Viktor E. Frankl, Professor of Psychiatry at the University of Vienna, says: "The greatest drive in life is meaning." In his opinion, the deepest desire in the human heart demanding fulfillment is a sense of meaning in living. "Not the will to pleasure à la Freud, but the will to meaning," declares Frankl, "is the deepest need of the human heart." So "goals are absolutely essential," the Austrian psychiatrist tells us. "For goals give meaning to living." Will they not create anxiety? Yes, perhaps they will. But this anxiety and tension can be the constructive motivating power in our life.

If the goal-pursuing human being experiences some times of mental unpleasantness like "worry" or "tensions" or "anxiety," at least he is alive. But the goalless or goal-arrived human being will suffer a far worse fate: boredom. And that is a living death.

Goals are not only absolutely necessary to motivate us. They are essential to really keep us alive.

**Not having a goal
is more to be feared
than not reaching a goal.**

---

2. *IMAGINE A VARIETY OF POSSIBLE WAYS TO REACH YOUR GOAL.* It is my personal opinion that a person should have at least three, and preferably many more, possible ways to reach his goal before he plunges. For instance: Is your goal to travel? How could you travel? Here are some suggestions.

1. Join the Army or Navy and request duty overseas.

2. Join a company that hires overseas workers.

3. Simply buy a ticket and go even if it means giving up something.

4. Save a small amount every day and you'll be surprised how soon you will have enough money to buy a ticket. In my student days I wanted to visit the Holy Land. I was broke. When I began my first job I simply saved half a dollar a day and in six years I had enough to make the trip.

5. Recruit fifteen people to form a party and any airline will be glad to give you a free ticket.

Whatever your goal, draft a possibility list of ways in which you could conceivably reach your desired objective.

3. *EXCOMMUNICATE FEAR FROM YOUR IMAGINATION.* Don't let fear push you down. It is amazing how fear will creep in as you begin to imagine yourself moving forward in an enterprise. No person is ever totally immune from fear and trepidation. At the entrances to some of the great cathedrals of the world you will find a guard dressed in a costume resembling that worn by Napoleon. These "Napoleons," as they are called, have the responsibility of denying admittance to those inappropriately attired. Once you have created some noble goal in your mind you must discipline your thinking, prohibiting that sacrilegious sojourner called fear from making his impious entrance into the sacred cathedral of your imagination.

It's amazing what fears can rise. None rises more quickly than the fear of failure. I suppose our church would never have been built if I had not read that one sentence on a church calendar:

> **"I would rather attempt to do
> something great and
> fail, than attempt
> to do nothing and succeed!"**

If you are tempted to fear that you might not make your goals, remember Robert Browning's "A man's reach should exceed his grasp, or what's a heaven for?" James Russell Lowell said, "Not failure, but low aim, is crime." Fear nothing more than fear itself.

4. IMAGINE YOURSELF GETTING STARTED. J. C. Penney said, "The hardest part of any job is getting started." It usually requires very little to begin something big. The first sale is always the hardest. The odds are great that if you will begin, you will achieve. For positive ideas are immortal. Even if your dream seems impossible—begin!

Richard Neutra told me, "I have never done anything in my life that did not seem to be impossible when I was in the beginning stage."

Begin by writing your idea on paper. Sketch an impression of what you hope to build, or an outline of what you hope to write, or the name of the business you hope to launch, or the dreamed-of title in front of your name, or the letterhead of the firm you imagine yourself founding.

5. IMAGINE GOALS BEYOND YOUR GOALS. Dr. Viktor Frankl said it:

> **The "IS" must never catch up
> with the "OUGHT."**

Therefore the POSSIBILITY THINKER holds in the back of his imagination goals beyond his goals. He realizes that he must never be caught in a position where he "arrives," and like Alexander "weeps" because he has no more worlds to conquer. Challenge and achievement are the very ebb and flow of the tide of life. Without challenge and achievement we are living as dead men. God pity the man who catches up with his goals and will not, or cannot, imagine greater levels toward which he can strive.

I have known the pain of frustration and anxiety when desired goals seemed unattainable. But the greatest pain of my life was when I awoke one day and found myself a success. I had arrived. All of my big dreams had come true. Happy? Yes, but not for long. You cannot live long in the joy of yesterday's accomplishments.

Unquestionably, my most difficult time in the ten years as pastor of Garden Grove Community Church was not the first week when I had still failed to find someplace to begin preaching services, nor the first six months, which I spent ringing doorbells, calling from door to door, trying to talk people into "coming over Sunday morning to the new church starting in the drive-in theater." I had goals, you see. First, to find a few, then many, who would help get this great church started. My goals were specific. Someday there would be a congregation of over one thousand members, with beautiful buildings, a large staff, a pipe organ and two choirs at least. These were enormous goals to a young minister of twenty-eight who had only five hundred dollars and only one other church member, his wife.

Ten years ago I was sure my goals were big enough to keep me busy for twenty years. Then one day I drove into the church grounds, after a vacation, to see the ten acres with towering trees, sun-drenched fountains and the great glass cathedral. It was beautiful. By now the church building had been featured in a score of international architectural publications. I found the other three ministers on the staff waiting to greet me. Enthusiastically I received their report on how well the church was going. Everything was going great. I was reminded that our membership had now grown to just under two thousand. Everything was wonderful. There were no problems at all.

I went into my office. Suddenly I felt the first onslaught of a depression I had ever experienced before. No problems. No challenges. No worries to resolve. No troubles to solve. Every one of my goals had been reached. I was lost. Don't laugh. It wasn't funny. I had all I could do to keep telling myself that my work was not finished.

**When you catch up with your goals
you are in trouble!**

I've learned now to have goals beyond my goals.

What Are You Hunting For?

One day before our church was built I parked my car on our newly acquired land. Orange groves surrounded the property. I was busy exercising my imagination, imagining a great church, fountains, towers, and bells. Suddenly I heard the crack of a twig and turned around to see through the window of my car a dark, bushy-haired man walking toward me out of the orange grove holding a gun. A shotgun. A double-barreled shotgun! Loaded! Cocked! I must have looked frightened because, lowering his gun, he said with a smile, "I'm just hunting jack rabbits."

I was never so happy to meet a jack rabbit hunter in my life. "Any luck?" I asked.

"I'm afraid not," he said. "There just aren't any jack rabbits around today."

"Well, there are six rabbits running around on the north end of this property," I said, directing his attention to the rabbits five hundred feet north of us on the edge of the walnut grove. "Why don't you go get one?" I challenged.

"Oh, I couldn't," he said doubtfully. "You see, they would see me coming before I came close to them."

"Well," I assured him, "they aren't running now. Why don't you move up closer. You just might be able to get close enough to get a good shot."

"Oh no," he continued negatively, "even if they didn't see me, they would be able to hear me." Then he got scientific. He went into a lengthy description about how rabbits were able to "hear" with the bottoms of their feet. Even if he walked very softly the rabbits would be able to "feel" the vibrations of his footfall on the earth. I was amazed at this man's immense ability to imagine failure. He was using his imagination to defeat himself.

"But why don't you just walk very softly, very slowly, very quietly, and probably you will be able to get close enough," I insisted.

Suddenly, a spark appeared in his eye. It was the birth of possibility thinking. He said, "Well, maybe if I try!" For a moment he visualized the possibility of success. So he began to walk slowly, furtively, stealthily, until he was within fifty feet of the rabbits. I watched from my car as he raised his gun, aimed, and fired. All six rabbits ran into the walnut grove. Dejectedly, he dropped his gun at his side. Suddenly he ran on into the walnut grove and a few minutes later returned holding a jack rabbit by the ears! He waved proudly to me, for he had succeeded in getting a rabbit. (Personally, I could never kill a rabbit. Perhaps you dislike shooting rabbits as much as I.)

But what are you hunting for? A job? An education? A marriage? A business? Whatever it is, you will never succeed at anything until you turn your sanctified imagination loose and imagine success at it. Honestly —there are opportunities all around you!

V

SPOTTING OPPORTUNITIES— SIX STEPS TO GUIDE YOU

It never ceases to amaze me how impossibility thinkers "never have any opportunities" and how POSSIBILITY THINKERS are always spotting more opportunities than they are able to pursue.

HOW POSSIBILITY THINKERS SPOT OPPORTUNITIES

1. *LOOK TO THE FUTURE—NOT TO THE PAST.* Be inspired by history; don't be trapped by it. "Anything we're doing can be done better—I have an incurable improvement complex," is the way one very successful opportunity-spotting possibility thinker summed it up to me.

Opportunity spotters know that almost anything can be improved: either the quality, service, price, packaging, delivery, merchandising, or advertising of the product or program. Perhaps it can be made bigger, or smaller, but it can be improved somehow, some way. Here may lie one path to great opportunity.

When we decided to build a "walk-in drive-in church" I called on one of the greatest architects of the twentieth century, Richard J. Neutra. I knew that Louis Sullivan, Frank Lloyd Wright, and Richard Neutra were fathers of the new and exciting international style of architecture. "Let it not be said that the most beautiful building ever built is the Parthenon. The most beautiful buildings ever seen by the eyes of man have yet to be built," I challenged Mr. Neutra. For we were a group of POSSIBILITY THINKERS challenged to do something bigger, or better, than had been done before. POSSIBILITY THINKERS are incurably obsessed with the creative notion that "the best is yet to be."

Be a pioneer and become a pacesettter leaving your fingerprints on the pages of history.

THE DAYS OF BIG OPPORTUNITIES ARE NOT PAST!

One of the most damning ideas that is going around the country is the idea that yesterday was the day of opportunity. The truth is there has never been a time in human history that held greater opportunities for more people than our present age.

A young high-school student shared this problem with me recently. "I feel I have been born fifty years too late." "What do you mean, John?" I asked. "Well, it seems like about everything worth doing has been done. They have a cure for polio. The land in our world is all staked out if it is worth anything. The car, airplane, and even rockets have already been invented. The biggest businesses have already been established, and the greatest financial empires organized. I feel I'm coming along too late in the history of the human race." "Why John," I offered, "the greatest is yet to be. Consider young men who lived six thousand years ago. They lived in that small civilized world called the Fertile Crescent, which consisted of Egypt, Phoenicia, and Babylonia in the valley of the Tigris and Euphrates rivers. At that point in history, some young man probably thought: 'I've been born fifty years too late! The world has now been explored. There is nothing left. Only high mountains to the north, great desert to the south, endless water to the west, and nothing but useless mountains to the east.' Undoubtedly there were young men six thousand years ago who said, 'I have come along too late. Look at the pyramids. Anything that is worthwhile doing has been done.'

"Today we know that civilization was barely launched. Centuries later the great explorer Marco Polo brought fantastic reports of a vast world to the East with jewels, spices, and perfumes and silks that men had never seen before. Today, we have yet to explore the countless worlds in space. M 31 in Andromeda is a galaxy three million light years from our planet, Earth. If we could build a rocket to travel at the speed of light—one hundred eighty-six thousand miles per second—it would take future space voyagers three million years just to get to the edge of this galaxy. Why John, the human race has not yet begun to explore this seemingly limitless universe!

"And if that talk is too far out for you, consider this. The bottoms of our oceans contain mines of precious jewels and rich ore that have not yet been discovered. There are buried treasures waiting to be uncovered, manuscripts of ancient history that still lie buried under dry sand in hastily explored Middle Eastern caves. There are vast world problems that we have not begun to solve, diseases we have never conquered, and oppressed people that have yet to be set free. John, the human race has hardly begun to live. You have come along at the best time possible. So far in human history we have accumulated a vast and vital inventory of telephone, radio, transistors, rockets, antibiotics, insulin, bottled oxygen, atomic power, and computers. We have the equipment, Johnny; it remains for your generation and the next to make the great exploits. There is a wealth of opportunity and challenge. The greatest is yet to be!"

2. LOOK FOR SOMETHING THAT MOST PEOPLE WOULD AGREE "WOULD BE WONDERFUL IF IT COULD BE DONE." When you find an idea that "would be great if it was possible," then you may be on the edge of a great opportunity. This is the time to remind yourself that nothing is impossible.

In a television spectacular, *Cinderella*, a player says, "Sensible people say it's impossible, but impossible things are happening every day!"

TODAY'S ACCOMPLISHMENTS
WERE YESTERDAY'S IMPOSSIBILITIES

Join the miracle makers. They are in every profession: medicine, religion, politics, arts, entertainment, construction, military, engineering, business.

A local newspaper carried a report from the Corning Glass factory in New York. Ray Wasson, an engineer in this, the world's foremost glass factory, holds up a slender glass tube, drops it, and it does not crack or shatter. "In 1963 our company spent fifteen million dollars on research for new strength for new glass and for new use for glass. That's a lot of money," says Wasson, "but if we don't keep trying to do what the books say can't be done, we will wind up making beer bottles and hula hoops." So, opportunity can be an idea that everyone agrees would be "terrific," but assumes "cannot be done."

3. LOOK FOR OBSTACLES, REMEMBERING THAT EVERY OBSTACLE IS AN OPPORTUNITY.

What others view as a stumbling block the POSSIBILITY THINKER is often sure must be a potential steppingstone.

Church management experts believed that starting a church in a drive-in theater was a terrible disadvantage. We suspected it to be a rare opportunity. We could imagine many people being attracted to a drive-in theater who might not go to a traditional meeting place. Because no one else was conducting a drive-in worship service in this area, we saw the possibility of filling a vital need. Moreover, because of it, we received a lot of publicity. At least we were different enough to be noticed!

Then the negative imaginators suggested that our small denomination connection was a liability.

From the vantage point of ten years I can report that what some thought a disadvantage was a supreme advantage. Our small denominational following was not a problem: It forced us to be imaginative, aggressive, resourceful, enterprising! Had we been unfortunate enough to have an immediate following of 150 denominationally loyal people we might have leaned back saying, "This is a cinch!" The perils of prosperity are often more dangerous than the perils of poverty.

Yes, POSSIBILITY THINKERS are definitely opportunity spotters. Many POSSIBILITY THINKERS I have known are people who had every right to be impossibility thinkers. Consider Stanley Stein. Stanley Stein has what is regrettably called leprosy. He is living in Carville,

Louisiana. He cannot leave the leprosarium. He is committed to remain there until the disease is completely arrested. He became totally blind. He wanted to die. One day something amazing happened. This possibility thought leaked into his mind:

What can I do with what I have left?

And it dawned on him that he still had his sanity. He would write a book! He would become an author. So he went to the library and checked out a book on how to be a writer. As he went tapping his way blindly back to his room with the book in his hand he met his doctor. "What do you have there, Stanley?"

"A book, Doctor."

"How do you expect to read it, Stanley?"

"I expect to find someone, sir, who will read it to me."

"What's the title?"

"Well, it's a book on how to write for a living, Doctor."

"Now, Stanley, that's a strange book for a blind man, isn't it?" the doctor asked.

Well, POSSIBILITY-THINKING Stein had his own ideas. Every obstacle is an opportunity. He would capitalize on his sickness by telling his story in such a way that others could be inspired to live above their handicaps. He would get a tape recorder, speak into the machine, and find someone to type his dictation. He didn't bother to explain to the doctor. His mind was made up! While all those around him were existing a living death of hopelessness, he had decided "to cast my lot with the living and begin a campaign to rejoin the human race."

He turned his unseeing face toward the doctor and

confidently announced, "I still have my mind, Doctor, and I intend to use it." And he did! He went on to write and publish his story in the popular book *Not Alone Any More*. If you could see this blind man walking on the hospital grounds you would see a man with transistor radios in his pocket and a portable tape recorder over his shoulder. So he communicates, writes, listens to music, and really lives. The secret? He summed it up this way: "Instead of bemoaning the things I have lost I try to make the most of what I have left."

4. LOOK FOR PROBLEMS.

Almost every problem is an opportunity. The old expression puts it this way: "When you get mad enough to swear, it's time to invent something." Success is finding a need and filling it. And what is a need but someone's unresolved problem? So look for problems. Many problems are unfilled human needs that hold great opportunities. Problems often are opportunities to sell an idea. Do you suppose we could ever have sold the idea of building a million-dollar drive-in church unless we had a very real problem that needed to be solved?

One of the greatest POSSIBILITY THINKERS I've ever known was Dr. Irwin Lubbers, former president of Central College in Pella, Iowa. The year after he assumed those duties, the great drought of the 1930s blew biting sand and dry dust into the plains, cutting off the tender corn and wheat in the farmers' fields, suffocating the income of the college. The school faced a terrible situation. Smaller men than Dr. Lubbers would have panicked. But to him every problem hides a possibility. He sensed that this problem created a grand opportunity for him to appeal to successful industrialists and professional people in the East. For everyone across America was hearing about the terrible Iowa dust storms. Dr. Lubbers made his appeal: "We have never asked anyone else for help. Even though you send your sons and daughters to the quiet Iowa town to be educated, the farmers have always gladly and proudly carried the financial load. But now they are penniless through no fault of their own. Will you help us?" Wealthy, sophisticated, Ivy League supporters suddenly heard about and wanted to help this "little college in Iowa!" How generously they responded. And that interest and support continues to this day, decades later.

5. SEARCH IN THE CASTAWAY AREAS OF LIFE.

Modern chemistry is able to turn almost any castoff product into a useful and profitable enterprise. Can you find something that is being discarded as worthless material? An accountant at a Midwestern meat-packing plant said, "The only part of the hog we throw away is the squeal." Is there a piece of property that seems worthless? A swampy area in southern California was considered worthless until an enterprising developer imagined channels dug to turn the swamp into a beautiful lake, with canals leading off from the lake like spokes from the hub of a wheel. He imagined homes built on the canals with a private dock for each homeowner. He has made millions on this idea. Think of the money made on junk, garbage, and fertilizer!

There was the gypsum mine near Grand Rapids, Michigan, which opened in 1907. It was a million-dollar plant employing hundreds of men underground until 1943 when it was considered "finished." An imaginative opportunity spotter named Paul Kragt saw potentialities here, for the underground tunnels had a constant temperature of fifty degrees. That old gypsum mine today is the very successful Michigan Natural Storage Company. The mine's easily traversable, well-lighted tunnels have been sealed off into refrigeration areas, and cooling equipment keeps these areas at zero-degree temperature. The entire mine is a very profitable and unique storage facility. Turkeys, apples, eggs, nuts, potatoes, pickles and beef are just a few of the many foodstuffs stored underground at the Natural Storage Company.

Don't overlook the so-called human scrap pile. Some precious antiques have been found in junk yards. Some of the best talent in America has been foolishly thrown on the has-been pile of humanity. Our National Missions Board retires, by arbitrary age standards, some of the most effective workers in the world. Here is where I found one of my most useful present-day staff members. Check over the pile of humanity that society snobbishly throws on the human scrap heap. I am convinced that

> **Almost everyone is an opportunity for someone!**

6. *ONCE YOU HAVE SPOTTED WHAT APPEARS TO BE AN OPPORTUNITY, GIVE THE IDEA A CHANCE, BUT DON'T PLUNGE RECKLESSLY AHEAD WITHOUT ASKING SENSIBLE QUESTIONS.* Conduct a feasibility study. Let the study determine the success potential of an idea before you put everything into it.

The POSSIBILITY THINKER does not plunge recklessly into every positive idea. So success-test these opportunities. Challenge all positive ideas by asking success-spotting questions. There are negative questions and positive questions. The impossibility thinker reacts immediately to almost every positive idea with negative questions like:

"What will it cost?" or
"Has this been our policy?" or
"Do we have the time to handle this now?" or
"Hasn't this been tried and proven unsuccessful?"

We have long had a ground rule in the Church
Board of Garden Grove Community Church that no
one is ever permitted to respond to a positive idea
with such suggestion-slaying questions. These questions are the heretical pronouncements of impossibility thinker.

However, there are four success-spotting, possibil-
ity-measuring, opportunity-testing questions most or
all of which must be answered affirmatively by knowledgeable people before a positive idea proceeds
beyond the dream stage.

FOUR QUESTIONS TO ASK

1. *WOULD THE PROJECTED SERVICE OR
PRODUCT FILL A VITAL HUMAN NEED?* It has
often been said that

The secret of success is to find a need and fill it.

Performing a needed service is part of the secret of
success. For that reason, modern industry will market-
research a product before it is manufactured. How
many people will want it or will benefit by it? Before
our church voted to plunge into a pioneering project
of building a walk-in drive-in church, we had to be assured that it would fill a human need. The reason the
drive-in church is a success is because it successfully
answers this first question. I am often asked, "Who

want to worship in a drive-in church?" Lots of people.

There is the woman whose legs were amputated just below the hips.

There are the parents of a mentally retarded child who can neither be left home alone nor in the church nursery.

There is the wife who has just lost her husband. Now she cannot enter into the church building without hot tears running down her face. Embarrassed, she stops coming into the church. Sitting alone in her car, she can cry softly and privately.

The drive-in church is a success because it is practical and fills a vital human need.

2. *WILL THIS INSPIRE PEOPLE?* Human beings are attracted in great numbers to the individual, the institution, the idea, or the project that inspires and uplifts the heart and the human spirit.

Could we build a walk-in drive-in church and design it and develop it in such a way that the building and the grounds themselves would be an inspiration? The POSSIBILITY THINKER knows that beauty is a major source of inspiration. Therefore, we quickly envisioned the drive-in church as being a place which could combine the charm of the old Spanish missions, the serenity of the most beautiful memorial park, the tranquillity of a mountain forest, the spiritual aliveness of the greatest churches of our world. If we could develop the walk-in drive-in church along these principles, we would have something that would not only be practical, but very inspirational.

Now, the tragic truth is that many practical people fail because they do not want to spend money on beauty. Beauty is practical because beauty is inspirational. The successful person is one who realizes that money spent on sweeping lawns, beautiful reflection pools, stately trees, is an expense that attracts people and pays for itself. For people are attracted to any-thing that is beautiful. Richard J. Neutra, in his book *Life and Shape*, put it this way: "Cutting the trees, putting low cost blacktop or glaring cement where there used to be grass to be watered every so often, is not practical. For it offends the eye and the subcon-scious desire for beauty more than people realize. We must educate ourselves to admit that there is nothing more practical or realistic than wholesome life. And wholesome life demands beauty and loveliness."

3. *CAN THIS PROJECT BE DONE IN AN EXCEL-LENT WAY OR AN OUTSTANDING WAY?* Not long ago I stopped in a shoe store in Como, Italy. I asked the proprietor, "How's business?" His eyes spar-kled. His face radiated joy, energy and enthusiasm as he said, "Great! Perfect! Because our shoes are the best!" And without giving me a chance to challenge the statement, he continued, "When you have some-thing that is pretty good, you've got something that is difficult to sell. But when you've got the best and you know it, it is no job to sell it." Excellence is one key to success.

A POSSIBILITY THINKING member of my congregation who is now in her eighties used to bake cakes in the state and county fairs. Again and again she ran off with first prize in almost every division. Her secret? "My idea of life is to do everything just a little better than anybody else is doing it," she said. Excellence succeeds because excellence attracts attention. The day America made its first soft landing on the moon, several months after Russia had landed their cameras there, a prominent American scientist said, "It's not getting there first that counts—it's getting there best."

In our intensely competitive society, the average American is so busy he does not have time to think. If you want to get his attention, you have to impress him. Often the only way to impress him is to do something outstanding. If it is the biggest, or the smallest; the most expensive, or the cheapest; the first of its kind, or the oldest in existence; in one way or another you have to have something that excels. I have advised all the members of my staff that I will listen to any suggestion as long as there is a superlative in it.

"Think big—big ideas have a far greater chance of success" is a familiar axiom. We discovered in our ten-year history that it is easier to raise a million dollars for a Tower of Hope than it is to raise eighteen hundred dollars for a new dishwasher in the kitchen.

But bigness does not automatically guarantee success. The dinosaur was the biggest land animal, but he has failed. A Chinese proverb has this warning against bigness for bigness' sake: "In shallow waters dragons become the sport of shrimps." When big ideas succeed, it is because they were also practical, or inspirational as well as exceptional. Bigness for bigness' sake is dangerous. The key word is excellence. Can this project be both monumental and instrumental? An idea that is both glamorous and practical seldom fails.

4. *IS THIS REALLY DIFFERENT? IS THIS THE FIRST TIME IT HAS EVER BEEN DONE? DOES IT HAVE PACE-SETTING POTENTIAL?* Almost anything that is being done can be done differently and better. Make it different and make it outstanding. In a highly competitive world, success comes to the exceptional if the exceptional is excellent. Be different, be practical, be inspirational and you will wind up developing something that's an exceptional success. Be a pace-setter. Develop a coveted reputation as the type of institution or individual that is the first to come out

with a new, exciting, practical, and beautiful program, proposal, project, or package.

By the time some of you read this book we will have built the tallest church tower in California. When we envisioned a great church development on our ten-acre parcel, we could see that the proportions of the property dictated the desirability of having a tall tower in connection with the church. "So let's plan our major church tower about two hundred and fifty feet high," we thought. Now, this was an exciting idea that had to pass the four-question test. Would this be practical? Would a two-hundred and fifty foot tower really fill a vital human need? Or would it be merely a tall monument to support a squeaky bell at the top with pigeons roosting on the roof? If the monument could also be an instrument, then it would be worthy of serious consideration.

I remember someone who was quick to say, "There is no way we can ever justify such a tall tower. It simply is not practical." I could not agree. What if we put elevators in it? Could we not have a chapel on the top floor? Would this not be a great inspiration to worship high above the sounds and sights of the world? Our sacramental imagination went to work to provide positive answers to all four questions. Yes, we could use high-speed elevators and divide the tower into 25,000 square feet of functional, quiet offices and classrooms, with facilities for a psychological clinic, besides a board room high enough so the directors of the church in their idea-generating and decision-making moments would not be cloistered in a paneled vision-restricting office, but would be high in the sky, unable to avoid seeing around and below them the lights of hundreds of thousands of cars, homes, and offices. Instinctively they would be forced to see far, think big, aim high, and reach wide.

The idea was accepted. The plan was approved. For suddenly the tower was (1) practical, (2) inspirational, (3) excellent (it would be for a time at least the tallest tower in the county), (4) different Churches have used tower space before for offices, but never has a beautiful church tower been designed in the international style of architecture as a functional office, chapel, administrative, inspirational facility from the bottom to the very top! It will prove, unquestionably, to be a pace-setting project.

The right questions were asked. The idea passed the four-way success-spotting test. We were convinced that this was another fabulous opportunity that deserved to be seized enthusiastically.

Somebody should have reminded me that once you seize an opportunity—get set for big problems.

VI

THERE'S A SOLUTION TO EVERY PROBLEM

If you want to seize opportunities, then prepare for big problems, but also welcome problems, for

PROBLEMS MAKE LIFE INTERESTING

Norman Vincent Peale tells the story. He was stopped on the streets of New York by a man who said, "Reverend, I've got problems!" Dr. Peale answered, "Well, I know a place near here that has a population of fifteen thousand people and not a person has a problem." His troubled friend said, "Tell me, where is this place? I'd like to live there." And Dr. Peale answered, "It's Woodlawn Cemetery in the Bronx!" Yes, it is only the dead who have no problems. If you want to really live, you must dare to live adventurously. *Every adventure creates its own particular and peculiar set of difficulties. You can protect yourself from problems by living a cautious life, but you may die of boredom.*

POSSIBILITY THINKERS know that problems are the challenges that will keep us young and spare us from the living death of boredom. A man who faces no problems, faces no challenges. The man who faces no challenges is a man who knows no excitement in life. He will soon be bored, and boredom is the only real old age and the next thing to death. The opportunity-seizing people who think big, talk big, and dare to try, will obviously create problems for themselves. The size of the problems will be in direct proportion to the size of the dream.

I recently seized an opportunity which created a big problem. Several years ago when Mr. Neutra and I were discussing our dream of a walk-in drive-in church, I said, "Let's design a church that will have the mood of the Twenty-third Psalm—still waters and green pastures." At the same time, unknown to us, a world-famous sculptor in his studio twelve miles away had an inspiration to create, in sculptured bronze, the Good Shepherd. So, Henry Van Wolf set himself to a task which was to take six thousand hours, three years of work, and an investment of thousands of dollars. First there was the small scale model, then the large model in clay, then the plaster mold, which was crated and shipped from his Van Nuys, California, studio to Munich, Germany, where Christ with four sheep gathered around his feet was cast in bronze.

Weighing a ton and a half, the seven-foot Christ was crated, shipped by boat to New York, and transported by rail across the United States to Van Nuys. Here, in an old barn, the figure was cleaned, polished, and finally coated with twenty-two-carat gold leaf. Coincidentally the sculptor visited our church and was greatly impressed by the still waters and the green pastures that border Garden Grove Community Church. "This is really where this statue belongs," Mr. Van Wolf said. "But a famous actress is coming to my studio today and I am sure she is going to buy it." I pleaded, "Wait one week so I can call the church board together and give them a chance to buy it." His answer was firm: "Reverend, I cannot wait a week. I need the money. I must sell it today if she will agree to buy. And I am sure she will." By this time I could clearly visualize the statue standing in the green pasture by the still waters of our church, an inspiration to hundreds of thousands of people for centuries to come. My opportunity-spotting faith was about to create a problem for me. The by-laws of our corporation state that I must give six days' written notice before a special board meeting can be held. But the sculptor would not wait six days. "Mr. Van Wolf," I offered, figuring quickly. "I'll buy the statue!" (The price was twenty-one thousand dollars.) "I'll give you seven hundred dollars today." (There was seven hundred in my savings account.) "And I'll pay you another twenty-three hundred for a total down payment of three thousand dollars in the next two months. And I'll pay you five hundred seventeen dollars and seventy-seven cents a month for the next thirty-six months which includes interest." "Well, Reverend, I believe that's where God wants the statue, and that's where I want the statue. I'll take your offer." And with that, we scrawled out a written agreement. Two weeks later Christ the Good Shepherd feeding the sheep stood reflected in the quiet waters beside the glass-walled Garden Grove Community Church. It stands there today. I managed to make the entire three-thousand-dollar down payment. By the time you read this book this imperishable, inspirational piece will be paid for with money that was voluntarily offered to me by people who appreciate the masterpiece.

One thing is certain—an opportunity means adventure. And every venture will bring its own set of unique problems.

How do POSSIBILITY THINKERS handle their problems? POSSIBILITY THINKERS meet problems head on with quiet calm because they have polished the art of handling problems masterfully. How? Here are eight basic mental postures to assume in dealing with the ever present problems.

1. *EXPECT PROBLEMS.* Don't be surprised when you run into problems. Expect problems and problems will not panic you. POSSIBILITY THINKERS are not starry-eyed dreamers who expect no difficulties. On the contrary, they are realists who expect their share of pain, hardship, and difficulties. So they develop a tough hide while they preserve a tender heart. Be tough on yourself. Give yourself a real brutal, hard, severe lecture. Nobody else will dare to tell you! Nobody else can say it and get by with it! *I tell myself when faced with dark times: "Don't be a baby—grow up—be a man!" YOU are the only person who can give YOU the stern tough talk YOU need to hear. Expect hardships.* The tenderest man I've ever met is also the toughest. His name is Frank Leahy—all-time great football coach at Notre Dame. Chatting in my office, his warm, gentle face radiated Christlike tenderness and toughness (a beautiful winning combina-

tion) as he said, "In our Notre Dame locker room we kept one sentence hanging prominently as long as I was coach: 'When the going gets tough the tough get going.'"

Because you know that problems are inevitable you try to anticipate the problems before you run into them. Smart people never seize opportunities without asking themselves what problems they might reasonably expect, always assuming that somehow some way, they will be able to find a solution to these problems. By anticipating your problems you imagine a variety of possible solutions. Then when the problem strikes you are ready for it. The chief executive is years ahead in envisioning problems and with them an imaginative assortment of possible solutions. Be ahead of your problems! No problem will ever run you down as long as you stay ahead of it.

What kind of problems can you expect?

If you are going to be a pace-setting thinker, then you can expect problems with people—especially people who are trapped by traditions. POSSIBILITY THINKERS may expect problems with people who have a natural inclination to resist change.

Every new idea will, in time, cost money. You may expect to encounter problems with people who do not want to risk capital, spend money, or make financial sacrifices. Be prepared—great faith creates great problems.

Is this the reason why many people do not really want to be POSSIBILITY THINKERS? Is it possible that the fear of problems is a major cause of impossibility thinking?

2. *PUT YOUR PROBLEM IN ITS PROPER PER-SPECTIVE.* Avoid the natural inclination to exaggerate your problem, an often fatal mistake of the im-

possibility-complexed person. The average human being has an amazing talent to make mountains out of mole hills. I remember a lady who came to my office to tell me, "I've had it. I'm going to divorce my husband."

"Does he get drunk?" I asked the troubled wife. "Oh no!" the frustrated wife said to me.

"Does he run around with other women?" I asked. "No, he's pretty good that way," she answered.

"Does he refuse to work? Or gamble his money away?" I asked. "No! No! That's one thing I have to say—he's a good man that way," she replied.

"Does he beat you or hit you?" I asked. "Goodness no!" She was shocked at my question.

"Well, is he a homosexual or a narcotics addict?" I queried. "Of course not!" she said indignantly.

"Well then," I advised, "be careful before you divorce him. I know a hundred lonely women who will really run after him as soon as you let him go."

"You know," she said with a sobering reflection on her face, "he probably isn't such a bad fellow after all."

A prominent businessman once entered the office of the famed Boston minister Dr. Phillips Brooks. Almost hysterical, the businessman blurted out to his pastor, "Did you read the morning papers? I'm ruined!" The wise minister calmed the businessman down and said, "Now just a moment. I did not read the paper. I subscribe to another newspaper. Half the people in town don't read that paper. The half that do only read the front page, the headlines, and the funnies. The fraction of the people that read more than the funnies will probably read the financial page, some others the sports page, and still others the woman's page. I daresay less than one per cent will ever run across your name. And those who do not know you will never be interested in it and never remember what they read. Those who know you will not believe it."

Guard against the overpowering temptation to exaggerate the seriousness, longevity, and intensity of your problems.

3. *WELCOME PROBLEMS, FOR THEY ARE THE REAL STIMULATORS TO SUCCESS.* They challenge the imagination. Every problem motivates the POSSIBILITY THINKER to think bigger, invest more money, spend more time, devote greater energies, hire smarter associates, organize a new division of the corporation, or reorganize the whole set-up.

Develop this attitude and you will not become tense, abrupt, irritable, resentful, jealous, cynical, or discouraged when confronted with problems. Know that every problem can exercise your imagination-generating muscles. Therefore, every problem can strengthen you. Be confident that if you keep a possibility attitude you will be able to reap profits from the problem. So welcome problems and they will not aggravate you. Rather, they will stimulate and motivate you.

Here's how to look at problems:

Problems are guidelines, not stop signs!

Big problems are not to be interpreted as signals to quit.

When she lost her husband some years ago this young mother decided not to surrender to self-pity. "Well, I guess this is my opportunity to go out and carve out a career for myself," she said. And she did.

She became an accomplished typist and was soon hired as a secretary.

All seemed to be working well for Virginia Hayter until her finger tips began to pain. The typing was proving to be an aggravation of a serious physical illness that goes by the sobering name of schleraderma. When infection set in the doctors she consulted advised amputation of several fingers from both hands.

I called on her in the hospital. I saw a smiling face cradled in the white pillow. Both bandaged hands were lying on top of the blankets. "How are you doing, Virginia?" I asked sympathetically. "Oh fine, Rev," she answered with a brave grin. We talked, then I prayed. When I finished I noticed her tears. "The only thing I think about once in a while," she said softly, "is what I will do if I can't type." And then, answering her own question, she said, "I am sure that every time a door closes another one opens." "I am sure of that too, Virginia," I answered. "I'll either learn to type with stumps or find a better job!" she promised courageously.

> **Every time one door closes
> another door opens.**

Two months later she visited me in my office. "Like I said, every time one door closes another opens. My boss was on vacation last week and the big boss was looking for someone who could do cost analysis. He checked the personnel record files and felt I might have a talent for this work so he called me in and asked if I would be interested in becoming a cost analyzer. He told me, 'You might lose your typing touch but eventually you can earn far more money than you would as a typist.'" Today she is very successful as a cost analyst. "Tell the people, Rev," she said, "that problems are guidelines, not stop signs."

Don't let your problems upset you—let them point you to something bigger and better!

4. REMEMBER THAT EVERY PROBLEM IS AN-OTHER OPPORTUNITY.

The late Congressman Clyde Doyle was a strong supporter of my church and a warm, personal friend. I remember a time when he found himself embroiled in a great national controversy. Because he was a member of our church I felt a keen sympathy for him when I saw his name unfairly attacked in the press. I asked him once how he could stand up against it, and he answered, "In politics we have the idea that even criticism helps us. The important thing to a politician is not, what are they saying about him, but are they talking about him. Even criticism is better than nothing. As long as people talk about us our names will be known. When the voters come to the ballot box the majority vote for a familiar name. Most of them still remember the name long after they have forgotten what was said about the man."

Another friend of mine found himself involved in a controversial issue for which he was criticized by the nation's most widely circulated weekly news magazine. "I welcome criticism," my possibility-thinking friend said. "It gives me an opportunity to reply to my critics. I have an excuse to make a public statement enthusiastically pointing out all the good I am doing, have done, and am planning. Without the criticism I could never have had the platform or opportunity to air my plans to so large an audience."

Isn't it wonderful how many creative possibilities lie hidden in every problem!

Speaking at the University of the Pacific in Stockton, California, I was impressed by the magnificent tower which guards the entrance to this beautiful campus. The tall Neo-Gothic structure rises stately and tall from a spacious green-lawned island immediately within the gates. It rises 150 feet into the sky—an inspiring monument indeed. Dr. Robert Burns, the university president, told me this remarkable story. Some years before, a water shortage developed and engineers were called in to study the problem. The engineers said, "The only solution is a new water tower." They insisted that the structured situation demanded that the new water tower be placed immediately inside the entrance gates of the campus. The thought of an ugly, monstrous water tank marring the front entrance of the university was a nauseating suggestion to Dr. Burns. But the engineers were unyielding. Firmly they issued the order: *The water tower will have to be built and it must stand at the entrance.* Perhaps this profane-appearing structure could be made into a sublime monument. The result? The water tower was erected. Around it, thirty-foot-square cement walls were built rising 150 feet high. Stained-glass windows were placed on the upper fifty feet to hide the water tank within. The lower two thirds of the tower were divided into nine floors and today house modern administrative offices, a board room, and a radio station. Few college administrators have a more magnificent view from their office windows than do the officials of the University of the Pacific. And few universities in America have a more inspiring architectural landmark to greet incoming students and visiting dignitaries than does the University of the Pacific.

Every adversity hides a possibility.

5. *DRAW UP A POSSIBLE-SOLUTION LIST*. Return to the exercise of possibility thinking, imagining any and all possible ways in which your problem could conceivably be solved. If one solution proves fruitless or ineffective you try the second possible solution on your list. You refuse to accept defeat. There has to be a solution. Perhaps you have to think bigger. Perhaps you need to have laws changed. Perhaps you need to invent a totally new machine or product. Perhaps you need to organize a new department. Be inventive in your thinking!

POSSIBILITY THINKERS are resourceful people. They follow the old maxim: "Where there is a will there's a way." One of my first experiences in the new city of Garden Grove was a meeting with six Protestant ministers. "How many homes are there in the city?" I asked. "Fourteen thousand," the Methodist preacher answered. "Have you taken a census of the religious affiliation of these people?" I asked. Amused smiles and negative nods answered me. "Let's get all the churches together and canvass all fourteen thousand homes and find out who is what and let's go to work on those who are nothing!" I suggested. Their response was not overly enthusiastic: "Make fourteen thousand visits? That's impossible. Do you know how long that would take? Have you thought what an enormous project that would be?" So that positive-idea-squelching question killed the idea then and there.

I mentioned my disappointment to a businessman member of my church, who was a real POSSIBILITY THINKER. "Fourteen thousand? Simple!" he said. "All we need is forty people who will agree to ring three hundred fifty doorbells. *My wife and I* will drive slowly down every street in the city, we will indicate every one of our city's houses on one side of a sheet of paper, thirty-five on a sheet. Then we will give every caller ten sheets, with thirty-five addresses on each sheet, for a total of three hundred fifty addresses to canvass."

Great idea! Two weeks later that man came back and he had every house number in the city listed. *He laid on my desk four hundred sheets of paper with thirty-five addresses on each sheet, a total of fourteen thousand families.* "Now," he said, "all we have to do is get forty people to agree to take ten sheets each, go out, ring the doorbells, ask two simple polite questions, check the answers on this sheet, and bring it back." So the call went out. The big, challenging idea of calling on the entire city in two weeks was a powerful motivational thought. Forty people volunteered. They came to a wonderful exciting dinner to pick up ten sheets of addresses. All forty left the Friday night dinner prepared to march out early Saturday morning. At the end of that first Saturday over seven thousand people had been reached. By the next Saturday every doorbell, fourteen thousand of them, had been rung. Forty POSSIBILITY THINKERS did what six college and seminary graduates insisted was impossible.

Unquestionably, there's a solution to every problem!

6. USE YOUR PROBLEM CREATIVELY.

> What you do with your problem is far more important than what your problem does to you.

Dr. Frank Barron & Associates have been studying human nature at the Institute of Personality Assessment and Research at the University of California. Dr. Barron tells the story of a young man interviewed at the institute. When this young man was an adolescent his mother became mentally ill and has never recovered. To make bad matters worse she lived at home much of the time. His father was alcoholic and inclined to wander, abandoning the family on several occasions. Furthermore, as a result of the depression of the 1930s the family was in extreme financial straits. Now, this background might be expected to produce a maladjusted person. On the contrary, the adversities of his youth had developed a strength of character that resulted in his receiving the highest rating in the institute's personality test lesson. Dr. Barron claims that *"personal soundness is a way of reacting to problems, not an absence of problems."*

Profit from your problems, capitalize on your crises, and draw dividends from your difficulties.

No wonder the POSSIBILITY THINKER maintains an amazing degree of imperturbability in the face of personal or company problems. He sees great possibilities of service, growth, learning, profit, or humor in his problem if he handles it right!

7. *CULTIVATE A SENSE OF HUMOR.* It never ceases to amaze me how people with intensely serious problems manage to extract some humor from their problems. Bill Bruin, a successful salesman, was one of the happiest members of my church. When he was told that he had cancer of the larynx he was deeply shocked, of course. He submitted to a laryngectomy, then learned to talk with a special electronic gadget. He capitalized on his crisis. He turned his liability into an asset. "When I talk with this apparatus people really listen. At least I get their attention right off the bat," he said to me one day. Until he died almost fifteen years later from a heart attack he kept a wonderful sense of humor. "My biggest worry is that my son might snitch the batteries that operate this thing when

he knows his Dad is going to give him a lecture," he laughingly remarked one day. He built up a terrific collection of jokes about his problem. He figured out a way to imitate a police siren with his electronic voice box. He had lots of fun with that joke. "People sometimes seem embarrassed when they meet me for the first time," Bill told me one day, "but that's their problem. I help them with their problem by making a joke or two."

8. LET YOUR PROBLEM LEAD YOU TO GOD.

> **No problem leaves you where it found you.**

Read this affirmation out loud: "I will be a different person when this problem is past. I will be a wiser, stronger, more patient person; or I will be sour, cynical, bitter, disillusioned, and angry. It all depends on what I do with this problem. Each probelm can make me a better person or a worse person. It can bring me closer to God, or it can drive me away from God. It can build my faith or it can shatter my faith. It all depends on my attitude. I intend to be a better person when this problem leaves me than I was when it met me."

There are many families in the Garden Grove Community Church that have been a great inspiration to me. Not the least is the family of Mr. and Mrs. Vern Dragt. While I was preaching from the sticky tar-paper roof of a drive-in theater, trying to get a group of people interested enough to help me launch a new church in Orange County, Vern Dragt was slapping wet plaster on new houses in El Monte, California, twenty-five miles to the north. One night he came home tired from a hard day of work as a plasterer. He complained about a headache but didn't think too much of it. The pain became more intense. His wife, La Von, told her two little girls, "Be quiet. Don't make any noise. Daddy's got a bad headache. And besides you'll wake up the baby. Remember, she is only six months old." Secretly, she was worried about her husband. After all, he was a prize-winning athlete, an exceptionally strong, able-bodied man who never got headaches. "I'm going to call a doctor," she said. Several hours later she received the shock of her life.

"Polio? Oh no! Not my husband! Strong men like my husband don't get polio, do they, doctor?" The next time she saw her husband, he was in an iron lung. Days passed. He lingered between life and death. Many people were praying for him but I was not among them. I was twenty-five miles away busily trying to talk a few people into helping me get a church started in Orange County. Weeks passed with Vern still in the iron lung. The meager savings of this young man's family were drained as expenses mounted. The young mother turned to God. She prayed. She found guidance and strength. "Well, I guess I'll get a job," she announced when their money was all gone. "No sense feeling sorry for myself. Let's go, La Von, and bring in some bread money," she said bravely to herself.

Jobs that pay enough to support a family are not easy to find for a young mother with no special training, no professional skills, and no formal college degree. Again and again job applications proved futile when she was unable to claim "experience." Then she ran across an opportunity to sell a product called Tupperware. "All I'll have to do is talk," she thought, "and I've got lots of experience doing that!" So she laughingly, but seriously and enthusiastically, decided to give it a whirl. She was thinking, "I think I can!" She talked Tupperware everywhere she went. She soon organized her business and hired other girls to sell for her. Debts were paid off and Vern recovered enough to get out of the iron lung. There were no muscles left in his arms. He could never go back to plastering. He would never play baseball again. Maybe this wasn't such bad luck, though. Possibly it was an opportunity to do something better with his life. While his wife sold Tupperware, Vern went back to the classroom and graduated in business administration. Today La Von enthusiastically inspires a force of six hundred salesmen and saleswomen while her husband manages the million-dollar business.

Some years ago the Dragts decided to move closer to their office—a move which brought them only a few miles from the Orange Drive-In Theater.

"Listen to this, Vernon," said La Von, reading the local paper. "Somebody's going to build a walk-in drive-in church! Isn't that exciting? It sounds like it is going to be big, wonderful, and inspiring. I'd like to visit this church."

She went to her telephone and dialed our number. Her call interrupted my train of thought. I was busy sweating out a cold challenge thrown to me only a few days before: "Where in the world do you think you are going to get the four hundred dollars to make the monthly payment for that land?" My secretary was out so I answered the phone myself. The Dragts became members of our church and their weekly tithe miraculously met the monthly payments on our property.

Today we are completing a two-hundred and fifty foot high Tower of Hope with the little Chapel in the Sky on the fourteenth floor—here the lights will shine twenty-four hours every day—reminding millions that "there is an eye that never closes, an ear that is never shut and a heart that never grows cold."

I remember how we challenged the congregation to pledge a million dollars for the tower. We prayed that someone would give $100,000 to pay for the little Chapel in the Sky! Some people laughed when we dared to ask for such a large gift. Nearly a thousand members of the congregation gathered in the Disneyland Hotel one night to pledge financial support to build our Tower of Hope. When I left the hotel at 10:00 P.M., the crusade director had two hours of auditing work left. It was nearly midnight when his telephone call awakened me and he said, "Reverend, sorry to bother you. But you have your Chapel in the Sky. I have just found a pledge for one hundred thousand dollars! The Crusade is a million dollar success"!

How astounded the congregation was when I announced three weeks later that Vernon and La Von Dragt were making a gift of $100,000 to put this chapel of faith high in the sky overlooking Orange County. That chapel is the gift of a family which learned that the darkest time in our life may actually be the blackness before a great new dawning. The little Chapel in the Sky might not have been built if one man years before had not spent months in an iron lung crippled with polio. "God moves in mysterious ways His wonders to perform. He plants His footsteps on the sea and rides upon the storm."

Got a problem? Turn to God and He may show you how you too can reap dividends from your difficulties!

He will even show you how to get the money you will need to get ahead.

VII

DON'T LET MONEY PROBLEMS
STOP YOU

It is pitiful how many projects are never born, or die an untimely death, simply because of the flimsy excuse "We don't have enough money."

There are many possible solutions to money problems. A ground rule in our church board is that when a practical, inspirational, exceptional idea is presented, no one—absolutely no one—is permitted to ask "How much will it cost?" until the concept is fully discussed. The members of the board will first ask opportunity-spotting questions: "Is this a need-filling suggestion?" "Would it be a great thing for God or for the community?" If it appears that the proposal would fill a need, or solve a problem, or create greater opportunities, or contribute to growth, or bring about fruitful improvements, then the question is asked, "*How* can we raise the needed funds?" It is assumed that somehow, some way, if the idea meets the test and we want it to be launched, we will be able to find a way to finance our dream.

1. *YOU CAN BEGIN WITH NOTHING.* Dreams cost nothing. Do you have a dream? Are you facing money problems? Remember this: All great projects begin with a dream. Projects can be started without a single cent!

> **The most valuable things in life are free.**

An idea, an hour in the early morning, a friend who encourages, the freedom to sell your idea, an article in the newspaper. All of these are free! So is talk. If you have a need-filling, God-glorifying, humanity-inspiring, imaginative idea, share it with trusting POSSIBILITY THINKERS and you will at least give the dream a chance to come alive. Truly, the most valuable product in the world is an idea. Good ideas magnetically attract support from unexpected sources.

2. *YOU CAN DO A LOT WITH A LITTLE.* In many parts of our country you can organize a corporation with only three people and fifty dollars. It doesn't cost too much to have letterheads and calling cards printed. So you can begin almost anything for very little cash. A little bit of money can go a long way to get a project on the road. If there is a corporation, or organization, dedicated to the fulfillment of a practical and beautiful dream, you can be sure that the human instinct to preserve a positive idea will surely move the project forward.

Could you buy a million-dollar piece of property beginning with only fifty dollars? I believe you could! You would have to form a corporation, a company, or a partnership to collect the investment funds necessary, but surely this can be done if the proposal is sound, sensible, exciting, and practical.

People are astonished when they walk over our million-and-a-half-dollar property and are told that it started with only five hundred dollars. But it is true. The tragedy is that impossibility thinkers use their imagination to dream up reasons why it happened to us without imagining how it could happen to them.

> **You can do a lot with a little that is totally dedicated.**

When dedicated leaders invest their best time, energy, and money in a project, they inspire other investors to come their way. Investors are attracted to imaginative, daring, and honest leaders. A young man with big dreams and a little money, putting all that he has into his idea, will find support coming from the kinds of people who can lead him to success. Halfhearted, half-cautious, half-dedicated promoters who are not themselves sure of success will draw little support: "A doubtful throne is ice on summer seas."

A young engineer working for an aircraft industry in southern California dreamed of bigger things. He saw himself making money in the construction business. A chance arose to buy a choice piece of ground with a down payment of two thousand dollars. He borrowed the money from his relatives, negotiated a construction loan, built a motel, and sold it two years later at a handsome profit. He then invested the profit in very expensive property across the street from Disneyland. He imagined a large luxurious motel. For want of funds he virtually built the building with his own hands. Many times I would walk past the construction site late at night to find Dick in his work clothes, doing hard and dirty work. He painted, scrubbed, hauled dirt, planted trees and cleaned up after the plasterers. For nearly two years he gave it all that he had. Today that million-dollar motel is ready to expand. The Jolly Roger, as it is called, is enormously successful. The secret? He was very honest, very determined, and very ambitious. He found that money came his way when he plunged everything he had into the venture. It is amazing how a POSSIBILITY THINKER can do a lot with a little!

3. *YOU CAN EARN MORE MONEY THAN YOU THINK YOU CAN.* Money should not stop you, for there is more money floating around than you realize. Just because you don't have it doesn't mean you can't get it. I advised one unemployed young man to become a salesman. That really scared him. "You mean go out and ask people for money?" he said. "Of course not," I shockingly replied. "Go out and give them a chance to spend their money. Salesmen," I continued, "make people happy for at least two reasons: People love to spend money. Go out and make people happy and you will succeed. Salesmen are bearers of good news, for they tell people about some wonderful product, service, or opportunity they might never have heard about. Many customers will listen, love what they see and hear, buy enthusiastically, and thank you for taking their money away from them in exchange for something they joyfully purchase. You make people happy when you help them spend their money."

I closed my short sermon by saying, "So go out and get some of that money. You need it." He seemed shocked by this kind of advice coming from a minister, so I added, "It's not a sin to love money if you want to improve society. The profit motive is a good motive if you look upon money as a means of improving your society, your family, your church, or your own mind and body. The love of money is the root of evil only if money becomes an end in itself instead of a means to greater service. So go out and get the money you need, John. Remember this about money: There are hundreds of thousands of dollars being harvested every day from the fields of free enterprise. There are millions of people who want to spend this money.

There are millions more who want to invest and loan this money. The man who gets the money is the man who believes that he can."

4. *YOU CAN BUILD YOUR FORTUNE ON BOR-ROWED MONEY.* Remember, there are millions of dollars waiting to be loaned out to worthy enterprises and to responsible and would-be businessmen. Consider the enormous wealth that exists in this country alone. The real estate in America is valued at more than a trillion dollars.

One of the greatest American success stories surrounds the life of W. Clement Stone. In his wonderful book *Success Through a Positive Mental Attitude* he tells how he became a millionaire using O.P.M.—"Other People's Money."

Americans have hundreds of billions of dollars in savings. These savings increase every week by the millions. Money reproduces at a rapid rate in a free and healthy economy. How many people make regular payments on life insurance policies? Life insurance companies have to invest this money. All money acquired in the banks and savings and loan institutions must be invested. If you cannot borrow from commercial institutions, you can often borrow from private individuals. This was the only way our church was able to finance its growth. Somehow, some way, you can borrow money to get started. Remember, too, that debt is not necessarily a disgrace. Often

Responsible debt is a badge of belief.

Debt is material evidence of a man's courage and confidence. Few successful businesses are ever able to go and grow without borrowing money. *Of course, there are responsible ways of going about this.*

Consider the benefits of being in debt.

Debt can perform real services. When you borrow money, many benefit.

- You benefit. You are given the chance to begin.
- The person who loans you the money is benefited. He receives income interest.
- The people you serve with your business or venture are benefited.
- You may actually save by borrowing. In many investments the principal payments on the capital indebtedness replaces money placed in a savings account. For millions of Americans their only savings is the equity they are building in the payments on their home mortgages.
- Interest expense is a tax-deductible item, another potential benefit in borrowing.

Just look at all the possible benefits that accrue when a responsible and honest person goes into debt. Often you may never succeed unless you have faith enough to dare to go out and borrow money.

5. *YOU MUST UNDERSTAND WHAT REAL DEBT REALLY IS.* What, after all, is "debt"? Fresh out of seminary, newly married, and just installed as pastor of my first church, I was earning a little over two hundred dollars a month. When winter approached, I needed coal for the furnace. I went to the coalyard and asked how much coal I would have to buy. "About five tons," they advised. "How much will it cost? And can I charge it?" I asked. "It will cost you seventy-five dollars and we will not charge it, Reverend. You'll have to borrow the money somewhere for we don't give credit on coal." And that was that.

So I went to the bank to ask for a loan of seventy-five dollars for coal. The banker gave me a valuable lesson in economics, "I'll lend you money for coal this time, but never again, Reverend. When you borrow money for coal you are going into debt. The coal will be burned. When it is gone, if you are unable to pay your loan, there is nothing you can sell to pay us back. When you borrow money for coal, or food, or the light bill, or the water bill, you are spending money that is gone forever. This is a real debt."

And sensing that I had something to learn, he went on to explain, "If you want to borrow money to buy a car or a house, we will lend you money. Then you are not going into debt; you are going into the investment business. If you cannot pay off your auto loan, you can sell the car, pay us what we have coming, and any money you may have left is your return from your investment. If you borrow money to buy a store and you borrow money for salable goods to put on the shelves, you are not in debt. You are in business. If you cannot pay off your loan, we can sell the store and the goods and if there is money left over after we are repaid, then you have a 'profit' from your investment. If you have no money left over after paying off your bank loan from the proceeds of the sale of your property, then you haven't made any money. It's that simple."

It was advice that was to give me greater courage years later when starting our new church. When we had our great dream of a great walk-in drive-in church, we knew it would cost lots of money. How long would it take for us to collect the money from surplus offerings? Perhaps twenty years. So we decided to borrow the money. When finished, the entire development was valued at one million dollars. Nearly $600,000 was borrowed money. Someone said to me about that time, "I hear you folks have a debt of six hundred thousand dollars." I corrected him. "Actually we have no debt. We could sell our property for a million dollars, pay off all mortages and have four hundred thousand dollars cash in the bank. We don't have a debt. We're worth almost half a million," I told him. It's true. We're not in debt; we're in the investment business for the purpose of performing a great service to God and our fellow men!

6. *YOU WILL ATTRACT MONEY WHEN YOU FILL A VITAL NEED. IT ALWAYS PAYS TO SERVE* is a truism the possibility thinkers keep in mind when they face money problems. In our development we reasoned that if we could borrow the funds, we could immediately increase our service, extend our influence, and appeal to vastly more people. The faster growth that would naturally follow the improved service made possible through the newly built facilities should more than pay for the annual interest expenses on the borrowed money, we theorized.

Our thinking proved to be accurate. The first year after our beautiful facilities were opened, we saw our income increase by an amount slightly larger than the interest on the total indebtedness. So the interest on borrowed money paid for itself in one year's time. In other words, it did not cost us anything to borrow money. Borrowed money resulted in increased public service, which resulted in increased income. We never worried about our so-called "debt." The expense is viewed as a necessary expense exactly as is the expense of salaried persons. It is when people suffer from "debt consciousness" that they are in danger. They're in danger of being more concerned about eliminating the debt than they are about expanding their service. *Improve and expand your public service and people will come, income will automatically in-*

crease, and principal indebtedness will very naturally take care of itself.

The downtown area of Santa Ana, California, is like the downtown areas of many American cities. Exciting new shopping centers have sprung up in the suburbs and the downtown merchants have suffered. Large, once glamorous stores are today turned into cheap retail outlets struggling to live. More than one merchant has gone broke. But there is at least one store in the old downtown that is doing better than ever. That is a hardware store operated by my friend Clark Dye. He founded the business twenty years ago. He bought the lot, cleared the trees, and built his little hardware store. And he never fell into the trap of assuming that because many people were moving into the areas his business would automatically grow (a fatal form of thinking that has caused the demise of hundreds of business places). He saw city growth as a challenge that could kill him or make him rise higher. He had the forsight to know that he had to keep ahead of new competition that was bound to come. Very early he invested heavily in tools until he had and has the largest collection of tools of any store in this county of one million people. His store has the most complete line of door handles ranging in price from a few dollars to—believe it or not—a few hundred dollars! No one in that business has an inventory of hardware that can match his. With a keen buying mind, a top sales force, and way out in front in quality, his store is where the buyers go. Parking is no problem because the other stores are so inactive that the streets are clear for his customers. Builders and developers from the southland drive to the old downtown area to visit this hardware store. Provide unsurpassed service and you can be a success. Once more: It is not a disgrace to borrow money to provide a needed service. It is a disgrace not to give a good idea a chance to be born.

7. YOU CAN GET THE MONEY IF YOU DARE TO ASK FOR IT.

"God helps those who help themselves." One of the most helpful sentences in the Bible is this verse: "You have not because you ask not." Millions, yes millions, of people and projects fail because they do not dare to go out and ask for help. Jesus Christ said: "Ask and you shall receive, seek and you shall find, knock and it shall be opened to you."

I had a visit recently from a young doctor and a young attorney who both belong to a small church that simply is not growing even though it exists in a heavily populated area.

"All we want to know, Reverend, is, why aren't we growing?" they asked.

"Do you want me to be honest or kind?" I answered.

"Honest," they replied.

"Well, gentlemen, I know that your church started when a small group of people broke away from the old first church because they didn't like some of the things the old church was doing. Right?" My callers agreed. I continued: "So your church came into being because it was against something. It only appeals, therefore, to people who happen to be against the same things you are against. You listen to negative, fear-generating, suspicion-feeding sermons and leave church weary in mind and tired in body with no enthusiasm to go out and win new members. And few people are attracted to a negative program.

"The answer," I suggested, "is to be positive." I elaborated: "Have some constructive cause. Let it be creative and inspiring, and people will be attracted." "But Reverend, it will mean that we will have to go out and ask for money, and that is what keeps people from the church," they warned. "Nothing is further from the truth!" I insisted, adding, "in our ten years of history we have had four campaigns for money, and in each campaign the attendance increased and we won many new members. Why? Because we were not asking for money: we were selling a wonderful, new idea! We were offering people an exciting opportunity to share in building something wonderful. Every person wants to be creative, important, and useful. The need to be needed is one of the deepest hungers in the human heart. And everyone wants to spend his money. Give people a dynamic program, and they will love to give to it.

8. YOU CAN HARNESS THE PYRAMIDING POWER OF TIME. Let time solve your money problems. Harness the calendar and let it harvest the crop of money that is being raised each year from the fertile fields of free enterprise.

I saw a picture of a man in the newspaper by the name of Benjamin J. High pushing a wheelbarrow filled with quarters. Some years ago he decided to quit smoking and drop a quarter in the safe for every pack of cigarettes he didn't buy. Now he has opened the safe in the wall and the savings fill a wheelbarrow. With a total of 10,130 quarters he is taking a round-the-world trip. Figure out some day the pyramiding power of money that is faithfully saved and carefully invested.

It's quite possible that money is not your problem, after all. Your problem may be a lack of patience. So learn how to harness time to let time make money for you.

9. MAKE GOD YOUR PARTNER. This is the key which may unlock your door to success. This does not mean that if you team up with God you will naturally be rich. But it is true that if you do enter into a sacred agreement to make God your partner you will receive insights, inspirations, bright ideas, and courage to move ahead when and as you should.

During a talk to a business group about our growth and big plans for the future, I was asked, "How do you folks dare to think so big and plan so big?" I answered, "What plans would you have on the drawing board, and what projects would you be talking about if the chairman of your board was a multi-multimillionaire? Ours is!"

Ever since that day when I surrendered my church to Jesus Christ and asked Him to run the business, the center chair in our board meeting has been empty. The center chair where I, as presiding chairman of the board and the president of the corporation sat, is an empty chair. The members of our board know that Christ is there. We believe that this is His business and expect to receive inspiration, bright ideas, and courage from Him. Who owns the cattle on a thousand hills, mines of ore that have never been discovered, and is waiting to make millionaires out of simple farm boys? Take Christ as your Partner and give Him a chance to work the miracle He promised: "I am come that you might have life—and have it more abundantly."

10. YOU CAN START OVER AGAIN. IF YOU HAVE SUFFERED FINANCIAL FAILURE, REMEMBER:

> **Fear is more disgraceful than failure.**

I have more admiration for a man who tries and fails than I do for a man who never fails because he never dared to try. It is a greater disgrace not to dare to try than it is to try and fail. "What if I go broke?" a fearful would-be businessman asked me.

"Well, of course," I answered, "that would be unfortunate. But if through reasons beyond your control such a misfortune should occur, it need not be a firm and final failure. Many people have gone broke but have not been broken. Read the story of most millionaires and you will find that many have been bankrupt at least once." ~

Don't let that old cry, "We don't have enough money," keep you from accomplishing worthwhile projects. There will be a way. In building our Tower of Hope we hired an expert named Bob Meyer. In two years he helped us obtain pledges totaling $937,000. So,

*WHEN YOU NEED AN EXPERT, HIRE ONE—
DON'T TRY TO BE ONE*

VIII

TEN TIPS ON TIME MANAGEMENT

If you hope to succeed as a POSSIBILITY THINKER,

NEVER   turn down a ripe opportunity with the expensive and impulsive excuse "I'm too busy."

NEVER   make a swift, destructive decision with the irresponsible excuse "I don't have any more time to think about it."

THE POSSIBILITY THINKER IS CONVINCED THAT SOMEHOW, SOME WAY, A SOLUTION TO THE TIME PROBLEM CAN BE FOUND

It is impossible to calculate the depression, defeats, and difficulties that are the direct or indirect result of time mismanagement.

HOW MUCH
- ill health is the direct result of careless neglect to take the time to have a physical checkup?

- destructive tension, anxiety, and depression in our society is the direct or indirect result of a person's inability to manage his time in such a way that he feels he has things under control?

- money does it cost industry because workers waste time, arrive late, and leave without completing what they could have accomplished in the allotted time?

HOW MANY
- marriages have broken down because the husband and wife did not take time to keep in close touch?

- students fail every year because they waited too long to settle down and work?

- partnerships have been painfully severed because executives failed to take time to keep communication lines open?

- penalties are paid annually for delinquent taxes or license fees?

- arguments are the result of tensions that mounted when a person found himself behind time?

- drivers die because they were too busy to take a moment to fasten their safety belts?

- lives would be saved in auto accidents if we only managed our time a little better? A recent study at the Stanford Research Institute showed that a little more time taken in driving would save the following lives over a three-year period:

* 5 minutes more a day would save 15,000 lives

*10 minutes more a day would save 24,000 lives

*15 minutes more a day would save 30,000 lives

*20 minutes more a day would save 35,000 lives

We must learn the art of time management if we want to live happy and successful lives. Many people are low achievers because they have never learned to value or manage time efficiently. Many others reach high levels of achievement because they have, by experience or instinct, cultivated the skill of time management.

"How do they do it?" "Where does he find the time?" we ask as we watch those fast-moving, high-achieving POSSIBILITY THINKERS. "I wish I knew how he manages his time. He seems to get so much done!"

Let me share with you some simple methods of skillful time management. Here are ten tips on time organizing that may make the difference between success and failure.

1. VALUE TIME LIKE GOLD AND LIFE ITSELF.

We tend to waste what we value too lightly. Though it has been said often, every successful person knows it is true that time is money. It can be invested or spent unwisely. Properly invested it is available to create ideas, organize plans, invent new products, study problems, or acquire knowledge, information, or experience, all leading to higher levels of achievement.

Perhaps we would treasure time more highly if we had to pay a tax on wasted time. Perhaps we would make better use of our time if we had to pay for the privilege of living. But time seems to come to us without charge—absolutely free!

A friend of mine who had spent years in a poverty-stricken area of Africa was horror-struck by the waste in America. He was shocked to see how we throw away tin cans, empty jars, boxes, cartons, wrapping paper, and ribbons. It is just natural in America to waste, and valuable time is foolishly consumed.

We also tend to undervalue and consequently waste a commodity whenever there seems to be an overabundance. Too many people seem to assume that they will live almost forever. There will be "plenty of time" to achieve something worthwhile before they finally pass off this earth. Thus the years pass and with them ripe opportunities.

Early in life my mother drummed this sentence into my mind: "Lost time is never found again." "Don't put off until tomorrow what you can do today," another old adage, is the logical follow-up. I was deeply impressed in my college days when I read the tragic lines of a dying author: "My book. My book. I shall never finish my book." So I began my lifework on the assumption that I might not live long enough to accomplish everything I'd like to. If I wanted to do anything worthwhile in my life, I'd have to hurry up. I have been in a hurry ever since. The first draft of this book had to be done before I left on a two-month around-the-world trip. For, I thought, I had to get this message out in my lifetime. The plane just might crash. Depressing? Not in the least! Rather, this has been the most powerful motivational force for rapid accomplishment in my life. Most successful men that I know are men who waste no time getting started. Get started early. Today.

Work each day as if it were the last. This will rapidly increase your tempo of achievement. It will also miraculously increase your energy supply. A strong sense of urgency is a great energy-generating force. Have you ever noticed how slow people seemingly lack energy, while those who treasure time and move fast seem to abound in physical energy? The fast-working, project-pursuing possibility thinker, with his high-speed thinking, stimulates the energy-producing sources that are in the human brain. Misused, disorganized, or mismanaged, it generates fatigue and weariness—first in the mind, then in the body.

So value time the way you value gold and life itself.

2. GET IN THE HABIT OF TIME ACCOUNTING.

A business organization values its money and demands an accounting of how it is spent. Nothing is more important, or more valuable to you, than your time. Yet have you ever made a careful accounting of how you spend it?

When people say, "I don't have the time," what they really mean is, "I don't think I have the time." If they made a careful accounting, they might discover that they could make the time!

I remember spotting a real bargain one day in Istanbul. I thought I didn't have enough money, simply because I had not made a recent accounting of my traveler's checks. So I turned the bargain down. Too late, I discovered that I actually had enough money. Make a time accounting—before you foolishly make a hasty, negative decision involving time.

Analyze your time expenditures. Get a notebook and keep an accurate record for a month. How much time do you spend dressing? Eating? Drinking? Praying? Reading? Body grooming? Cleaning? Reparing? Shopping? Visiting? Make a detailed study. You will be amazed at some of your hard factual findings. You will begin to understand the problem of time in modern life. You will discover that overly much time is spent painting, patching, pruning, pressing, packing, unpacking and repairing.

When you finsih your study, you may be forced to make some drastic decisions about your life. You surely will be better prepared to budget your time wisely and fruitfully.

It has been observed that time is a bigger problem today than a century ago. Isn't that peculiar? With all of our rapid means of communication and timesaving devices. After you account for your time you may find the reasons for this phenomenon. My father and mother lived in the age between the horse and buggy and automobile. Because they lived in the country and started life with the horse and buggy, they went to town only once a week. They made all of their purchases on that one trip. The round trip to town took one hour. They spent sixty minutes a week traveling to the store. How much time do you spend in one week traveling from your house to the car to the store, and back again?

3. *BUDGET YOUR TIME.* You know now how you spend your time. You know, too, exactly how many hours there are in a day. Start a time budget. This begins with a plan. Plan your day and work your plan. We have all had frustrating times when we planned

our day and we tried to work our plan—only to have unforeseeable interruptions. As a result, we may be tempted to give up and simply head into every day without a plan. Nothing could be more disastrous as far as your time budget is concerned. Unaccountable loss is inevitable. You will end up talking too long on the telephone, and compulsively spending your time in nonconstructive ways.

Make a written list of what you would *like* to do today, what you *can* do today, what you *must* do today. Now make a priority list. List first things first. Allocate your first minutes to those opportunities that may never come again. This will often take priority over what you think you "must" do. You will be surprised to find that many things you think you must do can actually wait.

Be prepared to defend your plan for the day. Discipline yourself against the temptation to top your priority list with what you would like to do. Strong self-discipline is required as you plot your day. Be prepared to say "No" to yourself and to others who might want to spend your time unwisely. You may have to take the telephone off the hook, or ignore the doorbell. Learn to say "No" in a friendly, frank, and firm manner.

4. *BALANCE YOUR TIME BUDGET* by your value judgments. More than one man has made a million dollars by working sixteen hours a day seven days a week for many years only to lose his wife and watch his children grow up and leave before he realized what was happening. Don't make the mistake of spending so much time pursuing your ambition that you join the ranks of those who are rich, but lonely; wealthy, but dead. The health of the body, mind, soul, and family requires that time be balanced wisely.

Remember that God created the human being with specific instructions to spend one day in seven for the rest and recreation of the body. Recreation of the body comes through recreation of the spirit. It is no coincidence that a vast number of the truly successful people in our world are also leaders in their churches or synagogues.

An anonymous Irishman wrote.

> Take time for work, it is the price of success.
> Take time to think, it is the source of power.
> Take time to play, it is the secret of youth.
> Take time to read, it is the foundation of wisdom.
> Take time to be friendly, it is the road to happiness.
> Take time to dream, it's hitching your wagon to a star.
> Take time to love, it is the highest joy of life.
> Take time to laugh, it is the music of the soul.

Look how one successful businessman makes time to draw wisdom from the greatest book in print. Richard Woike of Los Angeles, California, wrote in *Guideposts*:

One Sunday morning I did something which I suspect is common among businessmen. I was sitting in church with my eyes upon the minister in the pulpit, but with my mind wandering through the week ahead, examining the various problems that awaited me. Suddenly I felt that the preacher was talking directly to me.

'What about you?' he asked, his eyes meeting mine. 'How much time do *you* give to the Bible?'

'I notice,' the minister continued, 'that the average businessman has time to read his morning paper and his evening paper, his trade papers, his favorite magazine and books, and yet, somehow, he doesn't have time to read the Book that everybody claims to admire, but which few people have read.'

That afternoon I found myself still feeling that the minister had aimed his sermon exclusively at me. It was my birthday, the day I habitually make resolutions and long-range plans for my year ahead. This day, however, I had the gnawing sensation that somehow my plans were incomplete; that something was missing from my life.

Impulsively, I went into the living room and took the Bible from a shelf and looked at it as if I had never seen it before, aware that in past years it had seldom been more than a reference book for me. I realized now that I had never actually read it through.

I was tempted to plunge into reading the entire Bible then and there. But the mere length of it warned me against proceeding without a plan. Furthermore, simply reading the complete Bible in order to say I had done so was not enough for me; I knew the nature of the Book, and its importance, and I realized that if reading it were to prove worthwhile, I would have to gain something from it.

The minister had said he read three Bible chapters every weekday and five on Sunday. That afternoon I examined various chapters at random, and discovered them to be of unequal length; my own work schedule would not permit me such flexible reading time. Quick arithmetic disclosed that if I read three and a half pages a day I could complete the Bible in a year. Timing showed I could read this much in 20 minutes; I decided to add ten minutes to meditate on what I had read.

That night as I went to bed I set the alarm clock ahead a half hour. My wife asked: 'Early appointment?'

'Yes,' I said.

That was 19 years ago. Next May 19th, I will start my 20th reading of the Bible. I expect to learn as much the 20th time through as I did the first.

For many of us, early morning has proved the best reading time; the house is quiet, the mind is fresh, the opportunity to apply the Bible is in the hours ahead. It is a good idea, too, to read with a pencil in hand. Even now in my nineteenth reading, I still come upon verses, particularly in the prophets, that seem obscure; I underscore them to remember to check them out later in Bible commentaries.

Marking has also made the Bible a kind of spiritual diary.

One note reminds me of the day my brother and I had a violent disagreement about a business transaction, and I had made up my mind that we could not work together any more. That night, I had rehearsed a speech by which I intended to end our partnership. Next morning during the

Bible reading, I came upon the scene in which Peter asks the Lord . . . 'How oft shall my brother sin against me, and I forgive him? till seven times?' To which Jesus replies . . . 'I say not unto thee, Until seven times: but, until seventy times seven.' The lesson infinite forgiveness brought tears to my eyes. Later when I saw my brother I knew I not only had to forgive him, but I had to ask him to forgive me.

Another marginal note reminds me of a friend of mine in the trucking business who once told me he was thinking of closing out. 'I can't find enough customers,' he said. 'I can't keep my equipment rolling. I can't even meet the payroll.'

I was then reading about Job. I asked: 'Do you believe in God?'

My friend looked at me suspiciously. 'Sure.'

'Do you believe the Bible is divinely inspired?'

'Yes,' he said, still wary.

'Do you know much about Job?'

'I understand he had a rough time of it,' my friend offered.

'Do you know he was in the trucking business? He owned 500 oxen—beasts of burden. He rented them out to people who wanted to haul something, or work a field. As you say, he had a rough time of it; he lost everything. He was about to close out, too, when God told him that if he had any faith at all he would find some way to hang on.'

My friend asked: 'And that's what you want me to do?'

'I think the two situations are somewhat similar,' I said.

Three weeks later he telephoned me. He had been on the road canvassing every possible customer. A few new contracts enabled him to get a bank loan; company morale was high, the men were doing better jobs, things were beginning to look good. 'You sure told me about Job at the right time,' he said. 'How did you happen to know about him?'

'I read the Bible every day.'

'How in the world do you find time?' he asked.

I told him.

5. BE PREPARED FOR INTERRUPTIONS.

By all means, budget some time for delays and interruptions. The man who has an income of five hundred dollars a month is headed for financial trouble if he has nothing budgeted for unforseen expenses. Likewise, many people fail in time management because they fail to budget time for unavoidable emergencies. "Always allow time for a flat tire whenever you are going somewhere," my dad wisely told me. I still do.

No two words will do more to solve time problems than: START EARLY. Repairmen, deliverymen and servicemen will promise you that you may expect something at a certain time. Unless they have a long-standing reputation for punctuality, you will be wise in allowing, in your time budget, time for delays. If you do not, delays can prove costly indeed in missed appointments and even more expensive in the toll of destructive emotions inflicted on your mind and body.

Allow for delays and it may save your life on the highway—or your grade at the end of the semester—or your reputation with an important businessman with whom you have an appointment. Allow for no delays and you may become irritated, aggravated, and angry, all of which are destructive emotions.

Delays Are Opportunities In Disguise

Time spent allowing for delays and actual delays themselves can be used creatively. A friend of mine named Harry Johnson drives the freeway. He always carries a book with him, and when there is an accident and he is hopelessly tied up in traffic, he reads his book. Last year, using his waiting freeway moments wisely, he read three books. I suppose this is also a comment on our California freeways.

My friend Maurice Te Paske is the mayor of Sioux Center, Iowa. He sends every citizen of that town a birthday card. How does he find time? Well, he takes these cards along to meetings where his presence is required. When time is being eaten up by trivia which do not deserve or expect his attention, you will see the mayor signing his birthday cards.

Many possibility thinkers accomplish the seemingly impossible—thanks to delays that they know will come. They plan for them. They use the time profitably. A delay is often a rare opportunity to impress people. It's a chance to build a great reputation as a patient and understanding person.

One morning I was waiting to catch a plane from Grand Rapids, Michigan, to Chicago and on to Los Angeles. "All passengers on Flight 711 will report to the information desk, please," the message came through the loudspeaker. Another passenger ahead of me also heard the sad news: "The fog is below ceiling, sir. The flight has been canceled." I could see this very important-looking man grow tense as he objected, "If this flight is canceled, I'll miss my Chicago connection. I won't reach New York City in time to catch the morning flight to Zurich. And I must be in Zurich tomorrow!" By this time the well-dressed traveler was building up real steam. I caught his eye and said, smiling, "I'm afraid I'll miss connections myself. Seems we both have a problem." I added quickly, "And we both have a great opportunity to test whether we are big enough to rise above a really irritating and costly predicament." Immediately the tense face of the frustrated Switzerland-bound traveler relaxed. His brittle voice softened. His bristling, demanding, autocratic attitude mellowed and he said to the blameless aide on the other side of the counter, "Well, sir, see what you can do. Meanwhile I'll send a cable to Switzerland advising them that I am being unavoidably delayed." He turned to leave for a pay phone. Suddenly he halted, looked at me calmly, and said, "Thanks! Thanks!" Thus he turned a trouble into a personal triumph.

When he left, he left something behind—a very fine impression!

6. *WEIGH YOUR TIME CAREFULLY.* Not all hours are of equal "weight." An hour early in the day is more valuable than an hour late in the afternoon. An hour in the spring is more powerful than an hour in the humid summer. An hour on Monday may invariably find you at less than your best, while an hour on Wednesday may be an hour that normally finds you in your highest, most alive, and most dynamic spirit. Discover which hours of what days are the highest and best for you. This will vary from person to person depending on a variety of factors including geography, climate, and season. In Alaska, where the days are short in winter, and the darkness long, a person's emotional life will differ from the emotional life of a person who is living in Acapulco, Mexico. Find the hours of the day, the days of the week, the months of the year when you are at your highest efficiency. Plan, as much as possible, your most important work to fall in your best hours and your best months.

A businessman tells me that he never plans anything significant for a one-month period in December and January. "Two weeks before and two weeks after Christmas I know my workers will be operating at only a fraction of their efficiency. I never schedule anything terribly important in that season."

Richard Neutra discovered that the very early morning hours were his best hours. For years he has been in the habit of beginning work at four in the morning. Many creative people have discovered that the early morning and the very late hours are their best hours. This may be due to the fact that their subconscious mind is relaxed since it anticipates no interruptions at these unearthly hours. A creative mind produces its most fertile thoughts in periods of deep relaxation.

Weigh your hours. And you will discover that by reorganizing you can put the biggest jobs in the best time spots and can accomplish far more than you are accomplishing today.

7. CREATE TIME PRESSURES FOR SELF-MOTIVATION.

To protect yourself against the temptation to postpone and delay your projects, create your own pressure system. You can do this by announcing your intention to accomplish something. Tell enough people that you are going to do something and it will not be long before you will have to begin.

Set time-goals for yourself. Commit yourself to a schedule. It will limit your freedom, but it will press you to get the job done.

Low achievers have a habit of safely protecting themselves from the pressures of schedules by not making them. The truth is that you may have to follow concrete steps to force yourself to action.

(1) Pick a concrete goal you hope to reach. If you don't, you will spend all of your life filing, looking through the file for what you filed, reading and filing some more, studying and researching and filing your observations, preparing reports on what you have filed and what you have researched, making indexes to your files and carbon copies for all members of the office, etc., etc., etc. It is amazing how much time can be spent doing the really non-constructive activities you think important. The only way to escape the trap of trivial time-consuming activity is to have in front of you a very specific, precise objective.

(2) Set a deadline for reaching your goal.

(3) Publicize your intentions and time-schedule to family, friends, and associates. This takes nerve. You

run the risk of embarrassment if you do not make your goal or keep your schedule.

(4) Once you have picked the goal, set a timetable for its achievement, and publicize it, you have created pressure on yourself. Result? You will get the job done! If not exactly in the announced time—shortly thereafter.

8. *CHALLENGE YOUR TIME EXCUSES*. Before

you turn down an invitation or an opportunity because you are too busy, analyze in depth your reasoning. You may not even be thinking. You may only be feeling. The truth is we all can find time for almost anything we really want to do. When something of overpowering importance comes your way, it is amazing how you can change your plan, shift your schedule and cut out of your life activities which you thought were so important the day before. Are you sure you don't have the time? Perhaps you are basically afraid of involvement or failure. Perhaps you are fatigued. And in your depression it may be your negative emotions talking as you mutter, "I can't—I'm too busy." Remember, you may continue to feel weary until you say "Yes," and try. You will continue to be tired as long as you are unexcited about anything. And the way to get excited about anything is to get involved. Are you too busy or are you too tired? If you are too tired, read the next chapter on "The Source of Youthful Energy."

9. *WATCH THOSE TIMESAVERS*. Have you won-

dered why, in this age of timesaving machinery, we seem to have more problems than ever?

My wife claims that some of her problem stems from the fact that we have purchased so many time-saving devices that she thinks she has more time than she really has, and plans too many activities. She claims (and I am listening) that her husband expects her to accomplish an enormous amount of work in the home and in the community because of these devices.

But this multiplicity of mechanical equipment doesn't always save time. The extra car means that more trips will be made; you are continually tempted to "quickly run out a minute." Of course you must change your clothes, find your keys (where did I put them?), locate the billfold or the checkbook, lock the doors, walk to the car, drive, find a parking place, walk into the store, wait to be helped, take time to be friendly, walk back to the car, drive home, park, re-enter the house or office, and perhaps change back into working clothes. What started out to be "just a minute" turned out to be half an hour. Has this ever happened to you? How often? So watch those "just a minutes." Consider the telephone. What started out as an impulsive call may turn out to be a ten- or twenty-minute conversation; it may open a Pandora's box of additional time-consuming commitments easily avoided if you had not called in the first place unless the call was essential.

Watch those timesavers. The toaster, automatic washer, dishwasher, vacuum cleaner, and automobile all seem to break down at the same time. An enormous amount of time can be spent finding someone to service them, visiting the repair shop, picking them up after they have been repaired, and probably returning them if they have not been properly fixed. Unquestionably, timesavers are often timesavers. But don't be fooled. Don't overestimate the time they save. They may be more laborsaving than timesaving.

10. *EXTEND YOUR TIME BY EXTENDING YOURSELF.* Often the time problem is simply the result of small thinking. We think we have to do every-

thing ourselves. We resist turning responsibility over to others. We find it difficult to find someone else to do some of our work. As a result, we are too often too busy to think through our problems intelligently, face opportunities decisively, and really live successfully.

I recall a marriage-counseling case involving a family with several children. The household was in a turmoil. The wife was exhausted, which made her, and the rest of the family, irritated and short-tempered. My analysis was simple. She was overworked. The answer? A maid. They had the money but, believe it or not, that common-sense prescription had never been considered by either the wife or the husband. How the wife resisted! She could not imagine anyone else ironing her husband's shirts or cooking their meals. The thought of anyone else caring for her children occasionally was unthinkable. Finally she saw the wisdom of the counsel, accepted it, and they are now a happier family group.

WHATEVER YOU DO, NEVER TURN AWAY FROM A RICH OPPORTUNITY BECAUSE YOU DON'T HAVE THE TIME TO PURSUE IT

Everyone—housewives, salesmen, laborers, students —can learn something from successful business executives by facing opportunities with these time-organizing questions:

1. Is this a good idea?
   . . . . If so, we must find time to pursue it.
2. Am I the person to do this job?
   . . . . If I am the best person to pursue the idea, tackle the new job, or launch the new venture, then:
3. How can I find the time?
   . . . . I begin with the assumption that I can make the time simply by:

- taking a fresh accounting of my daily minutes.
- checking to see if any of my present time-consuming activities can be eliminated, postponed, speeded up, or assigned to another person or even a new machine.
- asking myself if I can begin earlier in the morning or work later at night.
- making an up-to-date priority list for my minutes in light of this fresh opportunity. What was high on my priority list yesterday may drop lower in light of this new development.
- questioning thoughtfully: Can I be temporarily or permanently replaced from part or all of my time-consuming tasks to study and pursue this project?

4. Is this something that I should assign to someone else?

. . . . If this new venture requires someone with less training or talent than I have, or if it requires someone with more skill or stature than I have—in short, if there is someone else who could do a better job than I—then it may be wise to hire someone else to do the job.

5. How long will this opportunity last?

. . . . Would it be wise or costly to wait?

Be strong enough to change your well-laid plans and your announced schedule if the situation seems to warrant it. If the situation demands action—then it may now be time to hire a man or machine to

make the time to take the opportunity.

6. How can we find the money to hire the man?

. . . . Watch out for that "there-isn't-any-money-to-hire-more-men" trap. A good man hired to fill a pressing need always pays for himself. He never costs. He always pays. You may have to reorganize your money budget as well as your time budget.

IX

THE SOURCE OF YOUTHFUL ENERGY

"Some people have more energy to get things done. Is there any way to get that added energy? How can I give it to others?" This was the probing and profound question a sixteen-year-old girl threw at my friend, Dr. E. Ezra Ellis of Whittier, California.

Do you suffer from a lack of energy? It may not be a matter of chronological age. A teen-ager can be explosive with energy, and thirty minutes later, when asked to do something he dislikes, you will see the muscles sag, vitality drain out, and energy mysteriously disappear. I called on a woman nearly eighty years old who was very tired. Her face, legs, arms, all showed that dragged look of weariness. "I have some good news for you," I said. She perked up. "What is it?" Even as she asked the question I saw energy come into the tired body. Eyes widened. Lips came alive as they parted to ask me her hopeful question. Energy was quietly flowing into the body from the brain that had been fed a possibility thought. She was anticipating happy news, which was producing energy.

"I heard you are going to be having company from the east, someone anxious to visit you," I told her. Now she sat higher in her chair. Anticipation mounted and with it vitality, zest, energy, and physical strength. I told her the name of the friend who was coming to call. The strength that suddenly surged through her tired body astonished me. She told me later that in the following two days she cleaned her home, baked cookies, made telephone calls, and really came alive. Where did she get that energy? From a powerful possibility idea.

Possibility thinking is the great energy generator. For energy is generated by happy hopes and keen anticipations of interesting or exciting events. Remember when you were a child, the night before a picnic? How excited you were. How hard it was to get to sleep. How early you rose and bounded out of bed. Not long ago I was suffering from fatigue. I was in between projects. Then I began writing this book. I began to imagine the completed manuscript, the bound volume, and I have never had more energy than I have as I write this. No wonder that possibility thinkers always seem to have an abundance of energy. Hope-filled thinking produces great enthusiasm and

---

Enthusiasm is energy!

Get the success cycle started now: (1) Get a possibility idea. (2) Imagine it. (3) Become enthusiastic. (4) Move ahead and you will experience great surges of energy.

Enthusiasm creates energy. Have you not seen it happen? I have, in many a committee meeting. The committee meets for the monthly meeting. They think they have nothing to talk about. But they begin to chat until out of the aimless conversation some creative idea is launched, picked up, elaborated, developed, analyzed, until the people who were lolling sleepily now sit upright. The hands that were lazily folded are now clasped excitedly, drowsy eyes are now alert, sparkling—wide awake!

The mental climate of the committee is electric with

excitement, enthusiasm, and energy. Suppose at this point an IMPOSSIBILITY THINKER steps in, pretends a profound intelligence by imagining faults, problems, obstacles, costs, and ultimate rejection. What happens? Well, if he wins, the project is torpedoed. The idea is dropped. The bodies slump back lazily. Someone yawns and says, "I move we adjourn." And the tired bodies wearily leave. But suppose the IMPOSSIBILITY THINKER does not appear or is overpowered by the obstacle-busting, problem-solving, cost-answering POSSIBILITY THINKERS. Then the motion is made to go ahead. When the meeting adjourns the committee members, with strong step and youthful energy, leave with a fast pace.

POSSIBILITY THINKING is the great source and secret of youthful energy. Why do we speak of youthful energy? Is it not because some young people, by virtue of their years, can see greater possibilities for achievement and service than a man who is calendar-old? This is the reason why young people without goals and dreams are really old and tired. They often have to do something unpleasant or wrong to create enough excitement to generate enough energy to really feel alive. This explains why some people in their eighties may demonstrate more energy than some twenty-year-olds. The eighty-year-old man with a constructive project has far more physical energy than the teen-ager who is aimless, causeless, project-less, and purposeless. POSSIBILITY THINKING generates energy. IMPOSSIBILITY THINKING generates fatigue. It is that simple.

So the POSSIBILITY THINKER, no matter how physically weary he feels at the moment, never responds to a positive idea with: "I'm too tired." Never! He responds with: "Is it a good idea?" And if he gets an affirmative answer to that question, he suddenly finds energy coming *mysteriously* from—*he doesn't know where!*

The truth is, POSSIBILITY THINKERS are people who have discovered the secret and source of youthful energy.

POSSIBILITY THINKERS may be found in every age bracket. I have known POSSIBILITY THINKERS of four and others over ninety. Both seemed to have that amazing quality of life we call youthfulness. Youthful people are keen, sharp, alive to the possibilities in life.

POSSIBILITY THINKERS are people who have broken the time barrier. When they are together they seem unconscious of differences in calendar age. They are attracted to each other by their mutual dreams, aspirations, projects, plans, interests, and hobbies.

I see them talking together in a circle on our church grounds—a thirteen-year-old girl, a seventy-five-year-old man, a seventy-one-year-old woman, and a thirty-eight-year-old man, all huddled together in excited talk! Happy talk! Enthusiastic talk! Project-planning talk! They are bound together by their POSSIBILITY THINKING, which transcends chronological age. They are totally unaware and unconscious of age differences. In this moment of dynamic POSSIBILITY THINKING they have broken the time barrier and are living in another dimension. They think young, see possibilities around them, and imagine ways in which they can take advantage of these opportunities.

Attitude more than age determines energy.

I keep a letter from a fourteen-year-old girl who lives in El Paso, Texas. She writes, "Dear Reverend, I used to live in Anaheim and attend your church in the Drive-In Theater. I have now decided that I want to be a medical doctor. I will want to go to some underprivileged country, possibly Tanzania, and build a great hospital. I want you to tell me what I have to do to reach this goal. I want to succeed in this dream more than anything. I know there will be many problems. I know that it will cost lots of money. I know I will have to work hard. I don't care. I am going to do it. I just want to know what I will have to do to meet your church's standard for a missionary. Tell me what will be expected of me. Leave nothing out. I've got loads and loads of energy and I will not let you down."

There you have a POSSIBILITY THINKER at the age of fourteen!

Dr. Albert Schweitzer worked energetically and enthusiastically past his ninetieth birthday. His list of accomplishments and honors was long. He continued to imagine that there was still much that he could do. Until his death he remained incredibly active working on a manuscript.

Browning wrote: "Grow old along with me! The best is yet to be." This is POSSIBILITY THINKING! Because they keep envisioning new and exciting pioneer projects, the POSSIBILITY THINKERS never grow old.

The Reverend Dr. Daniel Poling, the elder statesman of American Protestantism, flew from New York City to California when he was past eighty. He filled four days in California with important calls, several preaching engagements plus business appointments, and then flew back to his full-time job as editor-in-chief of the nation's largest nonsectarian religious periodical. Where does he get his energy? Out of his imagination and enthusiasm! He sees so many possible ways to be continually creative and constructive. No wonder he looks and seems much younger than his fourscore years. POSSIBILITY THINKING *is the long-sought-after fountain of youth.*

**A man is not old until he has lost his vision.
And a man is young as long as he sees possibilities
around him!**

In the Garden Grove Community Church we have an organization which used to be called "Senior Citizens." We renamed this organization THE KEEN-AGERS. Though some of them wear thicker glasses than they did years before, they have a keener eye for loving, helping, working, in their church, on their street, and in their community. They are sharpening old skills long neglected through the high-pressure years. They are finally trying their hand at hobbies they never had time for before. They are really keen on living all the days of their life. No wonder we call them KEEN-AGERS.

Recently I lectured on an eastern college campus. I was inspired by the POSSIBILITY THINKING of some of these young people. They are out to conquer the world. They have great dreams, high hopes, exciting goals. They are exciting, alive, keen-agers. At the same time I met some old people between the ages of eighteen and twenty-four. They were dull-agers. Though they were doing very well academically, they were doing very poorly in their thinking. For they were pessimistic, cynical, and depressed because they saw no hope for a happy future. Consequently they were lacking in enthusiasm and the youthful energy that enthusiasm always produces. They looked old. They acted old. They are old. For an old person is a person who has no future. And we create our future in our imagination. If I can imagine something wonderful that I can do today, or tomorrow, then I have a future! It is tragically true that some eighteen-year-old people see no future for themselves. They have no creative imagination. They are impossibility thinkers. They see only problems which, because of their unsparked imagination, they accept as insurmountable obstacles. In their impossibility-orientated imagination they are defeated.

General Douglas MacArthur, from the vantage point of his own ripe years, said in Los Angeles in 1956, "You are as young as your faith, as old as your doubt; as young as your confidence, as old as your fear; as young as your hope, as old as your despair. In the central place of every heart there is a recording chamber; so long as it receives messages of beauty, hope, cheer and courage, so long are we young. When the wires are all down and your heart is covered with the snows of pessimism and the ice of cynicism, then and then only are you grown old."

Unquestionably, some of the most damnable effects of impossibility thinking are seen in the widespread negative notion that at some mysterious point between the calendar ages of forty-five to sixty-five, a man is automatically judged as "having passed the apex of his career." What damage has this thinking done! It has created a morbid mood of "old-thinking" in the minds of some of our ablest citizens. No wonder some middle-aged men lose their incentive for living. Great minds, creative thinkers, experienced leaders are strongly tempted to begin quitting, just at the time when they are about to graduate with honors from the school of experience.

With the rapid strides being made in modern medicine it is quite possible for many people to enjoy physical soundness to the end. There may be some creakiness in the bones, but physical soundness will largely be determined by one's way of thinking. Your own mind is the fountain of youth, or the sewer of old age. Let's remodel our attitudes toward "old age." Let's modernize our thinking about "old people."

Dr. Henry Poppen, one of the most dynamic ministers on the staff at Garden Grove Community Church,

is over seventy-five. He is and has always been a great
POSSIBILITY THINKER. He is and has always been a
keen-ager. After spending forty years in China as a
missionary he was taken prisoner by the Communists
and became the coveted personal prisoner of Mao
Tse-tung. Finally his public trial was held. The gray-
haired missionary was led to a crude stand in the city
square where a crowd of over ten thousand people listened as he was falsely accused of every crime in the
book. It was not his first encounter with danger. He
had lived through three wars. He had faced, eyeball to
eyeball, the head of the Japanese army when China
was invaded some years before. People all around the
world were praying now for this famous missionary.
Their prayers were answered. The trial ended with a
verdict of "guilty." But the punishment turned out to
be "banishment forever from the China mainland." He
was given twenty-four hours to get out of the land.
Not long after, he was back in América. He was in his
sixties now. He had lived a full life, had been through
enormous ordeals. It was decided that "he should be
retired. The 'old fellow' has had it." It was true that he
looked pretty haggard, drawn. After all, he had been
through a hellish experience. I dropped him a letter
one day in Kalamazoo, Michigan. "Dr. Poppen, I think
you could do a great job for us in Garden Grove. How
about it?" His imagination went to work. Energy
came. And with it his promise to come to California
"to see if I can help this young fellow." Dr. Poppen
has already spent several fruitful years on our staff.
His energy astounds people. Some old people allow
the calendar to fool them into thinking they have no
more energy. Actually, they subconsciously suspect
that they can finally give in to the undying temptation
to take it easy.

> **The temptation to laziness never grows old.**

Another reason POSSIBILITY THINKERS seem to have such unlimited energy is because in their daring pursuit of possibilities they have escaped from boredom, a major cause of fatigue. What is boredom but a lack of enthusiasm? A great deal of boredom is the result of cautious, play-it-safe, don't-take-a-chance-until-you-are-sure living. These POSSIBILITY THINKERS are glorified gamblers. When they spot some unfulfilled need, or are caught up by some practical, inspiring dream, they commit themselves without unconditional guarantees against failure.

POSSIBILITY THINKERS are risk-running, chance-taking, high-adventure-seeking sanctified speculators. For they are more interested in service and success than they are in security. As a result they plunge when they see great potentials. Nerve and courage are the trademarks of their character. They have escaped the monotony that penalizes careful people with boredom, listlessness and fatigue.

> Some men die by shrapnel
> And some go down in flames,
> But most men perish inch by inch,
> Playing at little games.

This gambling spirit also keeps them young and energetic. The eager willingness to take a chance is a mark of youth. Young people tend to be daring. Old people tend to be careful. When the play-it-safe spirit takes over, age has begun to knock at the door. When the seeking-adventure spirit begins to wane and the seeking-security spirit moves in, you are facing the first symptom of decay.

New civilizations, institutions, nations, businesses,

demonstrate great daring in their days of youth. Witness the Pilgrims setting sail for the new world in a tiny boat, without radio, penicillin, bottled oxygen, or aspirin. Only a great dream! Or consider the pioneers that headed for the far American West. The trip would take months by oxen-drawn covered wagons. The dangers were enormous. The guarantees were slim. Courage ran hot in their blood, and energy poured powerfully forth.

The spirit of chance-taking thrives most in the age of becoming. Why? Is it because there is little to lose? It is easier to be brave in the age of becoming than in the age of arriving, for there is no way to go but up! There is always great danger that the valiant spirit will be lost when success is gained. At this stage there is something to lose. "I'd better quit while I'm ahead," one may reason. Some of the most insecure people I know are those who have no small amount of material wealth. They are afflicted with anxiety, worry, and fear of making costly errors of judgment in their investment programs. They are more afflicted with a greater mood of insecurity in their arriving than they were in their becoming. Having accumulated fortunes, they have lost their youthful vitality. Tragic! True as it is for individuals, it is a degeneration equally apparent in states, nations, civilizations, business, and industry. Few parts of America demonstrate more dynamism today than the Far West. California, Arizona, Nevada feel young, think young, dare young, for they are young.

One of the most energetic men who ever lived was Theodore Roosevelt. He was a daring POSSIBILITY THINKER who said, "Far better it is to dare mighty things, to win glorious triumphs, even though checkered by failure, than to take rank with those poor spirits who neither enjoy much nor suffer much, because they live in the gray twilight that knows not victory nor defeat."

Come alive! Find a dream. Pick a goal. Take on a project. You'll feel young again. Youthful energy will burst forth from the tomb of your half-dead body. You will be born again! Isn't that wonderful?

TEN STEPS TO REGENERATE YOUR ENERGY SUPPLY

1. *ANALYZE YOUR FATIGUE.* Are you sure you are really tired? Recently my wife and I spent a weekend at an ocean resort. "Boy, am I tired," I said. I really felt weary. I had been working at a fierce pace. "You're not tired. You're just relaxing," my perceptive wife said. "Of course," I sincerely thought, "this isn't weariness, this is complete relaxation!" And when my mind recognized this as "relaxation" instead of "tiredness," I felt wonderful. I wasn't tired at all. You will discover that much fatigue is really relaxation, or disorganization, or indecision, or hidden hostility, or boredom, or guilt, or frustration, or the trapped feeling.

2. *CHECK YOUR PHYSICAL CONDITION.* Have a physical checkup. Perhaps you need vitamins or exercise. I have found when fatigued I can actually generate new energy by taking a healthy walk. Walking is a lost art in our sit-down society. Exercise can generate energy. Perhaps you are overweight. This contributes to fatigue. "I'm tired of sitting," "I'm tired of standing," "I'm tired of carrying this weight around," are really very revealing causes of much fatigue.

3. *TAP YOUR UNDISCOVERED ENERGY.* All of us have energy we never use because we don't know we have it . . . until we have to use it! *Reader's Digest*

once told the actual story of a man who moved a truck to rescue a burning driver. Impossible? How did he do it? he was asked. His answer: "A man don't know what strength he has until he has to do it." Discover and draw from that vast untapped energy within you. How?

4. COMMIT YOURSELF TO SOME WONDERFUL CAUSE, PROJECT, GOAL, OR PROBLEM-BUSTING TASK.

Until you are committed you will be lacking in energy. The energy to do a job seldom comes until you plunge and leap into the assignment. The energy comes after you have forced yourself to begin. Too tired to begin? Then get started anyway. The strength will come. Hesitancy never generates energy. It drains energy out of you. Commitment—even reluctant commitment—is often the first step to eliminating fatigue.

Confused goals, indefinite plans and objectives, vague opinions, not yet firmed into concrete convictions, will leave you in an uncommitted and fatigued frame of mind. "I'm tired of thinking about it," you say as you seek to drop the subject. *Such fatigue may only be a subconscious defensive attempt to avoid facing and making a difficult decision.* Once you have forced yourself to make the painful or frightening commitment, you will find the false fatigue of indecision disappearing. Energy surges up as you dedicate yourself to your decision.

5. GET ORGANIZED TO ACHIEVE.

Avoid fatigue that comes from that overwhelmed feeling. If the job seems overwhelming and you don't see how you can handle it you will experience discouragement, confusion, and depression. Your mind, in a desperate defensive maneuver, will tell your body that you are tired.

This is a lie. You are not tired. You are simply disorganized. Throw the excess baggage out of your life and your time. Find the help you need, learn to say "No" to the trivialities and you will soon be on top of things. When you feel you are in control and on top of the situation you will feel strong. Energy will surge forth.

6. *DRAW CLOSE TO ENERGETIC PEOPLE.* When you are with complaining, self-pitying, negative people you will find energy draining out of you. Draw close to positive-thinking people and they will excite you. You will draw energy from them. "I'm tired of listening to his complaints," you say. Truly, negative people weary you. Likewise, you can be physically tired of listening to your own mental crying, complaining, and worrying.

7. *DEHYPNOTIZE YOURSELF FROM THOSE FATIGUE FEELINGS AND START HYPNOTIZING YOURSELF INTO ENERGY.* More than one day I began "feeling tired." I made the mistake of saying "I am tired." I vocalized my deceptive, negative emotions. Result? I really was tired. *I intensified my fatigue by talking myself into believing what I was feeling.* Now I force myself to say "I feel energetic. I feel energy surging through my blood vessels. I feel muscles in my arms and legs." I squeeze my fists tightly until I feel strong and I say, "I am strong! I feel strong!" And strength, energy, and vitality honestly do come forth.

Crazy? Not at all. It is the harnessing of scientific laws that cause the negative-thinking brain to "stop lying when it tried to tell me that I was tired." This positive affirmation unlocks enthusiastic thoughts, which themselves are energy forces; the muscles relax under this tension-relieving mental climate; relaxed muscles allow better blood circulation; and as a result, the energy potential within the organism is released. It really works.

8. SET ASIDE REGULAR PERIODS TO REGEN-ERATE THE ENERGY SUPPLY. Nothing will do this better than weekly attendance at an energy-producing worship service. Countless thousands of people go to church to have their spirits lifted. Lift your spirits and you restore energy. Strong minds produce strong bodies. "They that wait upon the Lord shall renew their strength. They shall mount up with wings like eagles. They shall run and not be weary. They shall walk and not faint."

9. TAKE CHRIST INTO YOUR LIFE. "The Lord is the strength of my life." "In quietness and confidence shall be thy strength." "I can do all things through Christ who strengthens me." These Bible verses tell us that energy comes into the life if Christ comes into the life. Here's how it works. Christ saves us from guilt. He forgives us our sins. Nothing drains energy faster than guilt. When you feel clean inside you feel young —and strong! Repressed hostility, resentment, jealousy, self-pity, boredom, loneliness, and grief are energy-draining emotions that produce depression and tired minds. Fatigue of body is inevitable.

> **If you think battle thoughts all day you'll be war-weary at night.**

Christ can cure you of these negative emotions. He fills your life with their positive opposites: good will, tolerance, understanding, helpfulness, and self-forgetfulness. These joy-generating emotions produce vitality.

10. *PRAY ENERGIZING PRAYERS.*

JESUS CHRIST, COME INTO MY LIFE. FLUSH ALL SINS OUT OF MY SPIRIT. LOVE PEOPLE THROUGH ME. I BELIEVE YOU ARE COMING INTO ME NOW IN THE FORM OF GOD-FILLED IDEAS. I KNOW I HAVE ENORMOUS UNDISCOVERED, UNTAPPED ENERGY WITHIN ME. I FEEL YOUNG, I HAVE ENERGY, I AM ENERGETIC. THANK YOU FOR THIS VITALITY AND STRENGTH OF MIND AND BODY. LIVE WITHIN ME, O GOD, AND DO GOOD WORKS NOW THROUGH ME.

THANK YOU AGAIN. AMEN.

X

THERE'S SOMEONE SOMEWHERE WHO CAN HELP YOU

YOU CAN ACCOMPLISH THE IMPOSSIBLE IF YOU WILL SURROUND YOURSELF WITH THE RIGHT PERSON OR PEOPLE

If you have a good idea—but lack the money, time, or knowledge to capitalize on your dream,

If you face a problem—but can't see how it can be resolved creatively and constructively,

Then the most important piece of advice anyone can give you might be this simple sentence:

There Is Someone Somewhere
Who Can Help You.

If your difficulty seems undissolvable, if your opportunity seems unseizable, if your dream seems unrealizable, don't become an impossibility thinker and give up! Be a POSSIBILITY THINKER and remember that the solution to a situation is often a simple matter of bringing the right person into the picture. Be willing to search heaven and earth until you find help. You may quit on God but God never quits on you. He has help waiting to lead you to success. You must be smart enough to believe there is help, determined enough to find that help, grateful enough to pay for that help, and humble enough to accept that help.

A prisoner in San Quentin learned this one dark day. No one ever felt more alone with his hopeless problem than Bill Sands did that day. Locked in solitary confinement, listed as an incorrigible, he faced three consecutive life terms. His father was dead. His mother refused to answer his letters.

Sitting in my office, Bill reminisced, "I asked her to send me a Christmas card. She didn't. I felt there was no human being who realized that I was even alive. Then the door to my nine- by six-foot cell opened. Inside stepped the warden, Clinton Duffy."

"Why don't you try to get out of here?" the warden asked. "Why should I?" Bill snarled bitterly. "Nobody cares about me. Absolutely nobody cares."

Warden Duffy leaned close, looked compassionately into the eyes of this lost young man, and with a tender firmness said: "I CARE." It was the beginning of the miracle that was to completely transform the life of Bill Sands. Instead of fighting the warden, Bill learned from the warden . . . he learned to live right. Duffy became the help Bill needed to gain his freedom. Three years later Bill Sands was a changed man and a free man. Twenty-six years later this man, once listed as an incorrigible prisoner, founded the Seventh Step Foundation, which has struck a spark of hope for thousands of convicts and ex-convicts. All of America is indebted to Bill Sands.

Wherever you are, whatever your situation, there is someone somewhere who can help you. That someone may appear to be your worst enemy. In reality he may be the very person who will prove to be your best friend. Is the warden the friend or the enemy of the prisoner? It all depends on the prisoner's attitude.

God has someone, somewhere, who can help you.

A husband and wife seeking a divorce learned this lesson. Let Henry and Shirley Hinke tell their own story:

SHIRLEY: Henry and I recently celebrated our twenty-fifth anniversary. Our twenty-one-year-old son heard us laughing and saying how happy we were. His voice broke in, "It wasn't always that way. I remember when . . . ," and he reminded us of a dark time in our marriage. Henry and I were married in 1941. We were both church connected and college graduates. Life was good. Only the threat of World War II loomed as a barrier to success and a full life of happiness. With the war over, we looked forward to our family togetherness.

HENRY: Without at first realizing it, however, the surging drive in our daily life had a new additive. The person "I" had to be satisfied. Associations were important only if they were to benefit "me." Sharing family happiness was ridiculous except as it exalted the ego "I." Tenderness was useful only to gain what "I" wanted. In the tough requirements of re-establishing a businessman image, compassion became a tool with which to gain self-acclaim. Although I was awarded a Community Service Key as one of Columbus, Ohio's outstanding young men, my self-centered ambition was causing real problems in my marriage.

SHIRLEY: Many dishes were broken in our house, as arguments, harsh words, and tears became the pattern. Several times, our young son requested a promise from each of us not to harm the other before he would close his eyes at night.

HENRY: If our marriage could last—and grow in love and happiness then no marriage is really doomed to failure. God is not dead. Miracles do happen in our present-day world.

SHIRLEY: The start of the miracle that happened in our lives was a realization that God no longer had place in our day-to-day life. We no longer went to church, and we definitely were not God-guided. This realization came only after the lawyer had been contacted and we were beginning the end. We not only didn't love each other—we didn't even like each other. *If a third person was necessary to dissolve a marriage—we reasoned—then why not try, first, a third person to save our marriage! We asked God to take over our lives and our marriage.*

HENRY: So we started attending church again. We were led to a marriage counselor on the staff of the Community Church in Columbus, Ohio, who really helped us.

SHIRLEY: This time, instead of just going to church, we became involved in vital religious experiences—really, for the first time in our lives. WE HONESTLY TOOK GOD ON OUR TEAM.

HENRY: We often open our Bible to read these words of Jesus:

Every one then who hears these words of mine and does them will be like a wise man who built his house upon the rock; and the rain fell, and the floods came, and the winds blew and beat upon that house, but it did not fall, because it had been founded on the rock. And every one who hears these words of mine and does not do them will be like a foolish man who built his house upon the sand; and the rain fell, and the floods came, and the winds blew and beat against that house, and it fell; and great was the fall of it. (Matthew 7:24–27)

SHIRLEY: The truth is: We have found both types of houses in our marriage. We are thankful, and humbly grateful, that the Hinke home now rests solidly on the rock of Jesus Christ.

HENRY: In the years that have passed since we made our decision for Christ, the winds have blown, the rains have descended, and the floods have surged around us in the form of the Korean War, more moving, a siege of rheumatoid arthritis, working for several years.

SHIRLEY: But through it all, we loved God as a family —and trusted Him to guide us. We had our frustrations, to be sure, but our love for Christ and for each other grows more beautiful every passing year.

HENRY: Since we really found Christ and accepted His help our home rests on solid foundation. No longer is there sand beneath our home to shift with the winds of fortune. *Someone asked us if this is taking the easy way—we tell you this is taking the only way.*

There is someone somewhere who can help you make your dreams come true.

Even if you have an idea and find the money and time, you can't build a successful business without assistance. John D. Rockefeller said it years ago: "I simply hired men who were smarter than I."

Find and hire men who are smarter than you are.

Your solid idea starts you to be a great success, but you also get the right men on your team.

Great ideas attract big people.

This means you have to be able and willing to work with people. Unless you face and accept this fact you will spend your one life lowering your achievement level. No man is an island. Even Jesus Christ said it: "I can by myself do nothing." Whether your business is building a home, a marriage, a career, or a business empire, your success will be enhanced if you learn how to be a team builder.

HOW TO ATTRACT THE HELP YOU NEED

"That company is just lucky. They have all the best men on their team. No wonder they are a success," I heard one failing, impossibility-thinking industrialist remark. I wanted to ask him, "Why don't you have some of those men on your team?" Why is it that some companies seem to attract the best men in the field? Is it luck?

POSSIBILITY THINKERS dare to believe that the biggest and best men in the world can be attracted to their cause. Try for the best man in the world and you can secure his help.

How do you attract the help you need? Here's how:

1. *BE PREPARED TO PAY FOR THE HELP YOU NEED.* Watch out for that negative money trap. You probably can't afford *not* to spend the money to hire the help.

I have seen marriages fail because a husband and wife felt they could not afford to go to a marriage counselor, only to spend far more money, emotion, time and energy on a divorce.

I have seen businessmen who felt they could not afford to expand, only to lose leadership in the field to an aggressive, expanding competitor.

I know a manufacturer who felt he could not afford to hire more salesmen. No wonder the company went downhill. Salesmen are the life force of an industry.

I know an administrator who had the imagination and vision to spot an opportunity, but did not hire the men to pursue the chance. He was afraid he "might have difficulties getting along with the added men he might have to hire." Today he is only half the success he could have been.

Be prepared to pay top price for the top men. The best men are usually worth more than they are getting. It almost never costs—but almost always pays—to hire the best men.

WHY ACCEPT FAILURE AND DEFEAT WHEN YOU CAN HIRE MEN TO HELP YOU SUCCEED?

2. *BE A TEAM BUILDER, NOT AN EMPIRE FOUNDER.* Today's executives build the names of their companies more than they build their own names. The average senior executive in American industry is not famous. He is successful but his name is not a household word. A century ago this was not true. Today's success men are not empire-building tycoons. Tycoons seldom attract, or hold for long, the kind of men that will build a strong base for their institution. Today's senior executive sees himself as the quarterback of a winning team, not the king of a vast empire exploiting, for his own glory, pride, and riches, the talents and abilities of his associates. Successful men are men who have a "team complex," not a "star complex." POSSIBILITY THINKERS are team builders, not empire founders.

3. *FORGET ABOUT STATUS, CREDIT, AND GLORY*. Status-seeking, credit-grabbing, and glory-hunting executives generate unimaginable jealousy. Instead of inspiring their associates to really produce, they stimulate negative emotions that contribute to a terrible production letdown. One of the most helpful sentences I ever read was a sentence I spotted somewhere a few years ago.

> **God can do great things
> through the man who doesn't care
> who gets the credit.**

The smart and successful POSSIBILITY THINKER finds joy in watching his associates get ahead. He never allows himself to view his associates as threats to his own proud position. He knows that this very thought will be the beginning of his own downfall. You can surround yourself with skilled specialists if you will establish a "share-the-credit-plan." A Navy commander told me, "We naval officers have a slogan: TAKE GOOD CARE OF YOUR BOYS AND YOUR BOYS WILL TAKE GOOD CARE OF YOU."

4. *OFFER THEM A UNIQUE PACE-SETTING CHALLENGE*. Promise them the chance to join in creating something bigger and better than has ever been done before. When Artur Rubinstein, the famous concert pianist, was in New York someone invited him to attend church. His answer? "Take me to a church that will challenge me to attempt the impossible." Great men are attracted to great challenges.

5. *GIVE YOUR TEAMMATES GREAT FREEDOM*. The greatest men are attracted by a great challenge

coupled with the promise of great freedom. Promise them freedom to plan, to dream, to imagine. Great freedom generates maximum energy and extracts unbelievable dedication. Imaginative thinking never gets started in a creative thinker's mind if he knows he has to "sell his idea" to several echelons of authorities above himself. Nothing stifles creative thinking quicker than the subconscious anxiety of having these ideas rejected by authoritarian officers or committees "higher up." It is true that some of the finest brains, and some of the most talented people in our country today, find themselves in freedom-restricting situations and would leave quickly if promised a working climate of great trust and great liberty.

6. *MAKE UP YOUR MIND NOT TO LOSE A GOOD MAN ONCE YOU HAVE HIM ON THE TEAM.* A businessman friend of mine said to me recently, "My manager has been with me seventeen years and the number two man in the company has been with me sixteen years." "Why, that is a wonderful compliment to yourself," I said. "How did you manage to keep them so long?" He told me, "I observed years ago that it costs a company a great deal every time it loses and must replace a man; therefore, I will not even think of losing them or letting them leave. I go out of my way to keep them happy. I am willing to make many and frequent concessions because I know that I can avoid the time-consuming and costly business of preparing to fire, then rehire and retrain new people every few years. As a result my business is tops in our area."

"But what do you do when they have problems?" I asked.

"I work with them. I try to help. I ask questions like 'John, what can I do to help you?' or 'John, I notice the job didn't get out. I'm sure there is a good reason. What is it?' I never tell them, order them, or command them. I try to inspire. If they still reflect some weakness, I tolerate it patiently, knowing that in a matter of weeks or months we will work it out without tension-generating discussions. I remind myself that any man I hire will have his weaknesses. I may just be replacing one set of shortcomings with another. So I try to strengthen my man where he is weak. If that fails I fill the gap in the job by rearranging and reorganizing."

What a wonderful team builder this man is. No wonder this possibility thinker is a roaring success.

7. LEARN TO LIVE WITH DIFFICULT PEOPLE; LEARN FROM THEM AND LEARN TO WORK WITH THEM. Some of the people you may need to help solve your problems or develop your dreams may be the kind of people who are not always easy to get along with. Learn to appreciate and work with people who, at times, may be disagreeable. Don't despair. Sometimes they can make life interesting. They are often exciting challenges.

These are people who seem to like to argue. Try to keep your differences with them on the plane of disagreement. Try to prevent these disagreements from becoming violent arguments.

TEN TIPS TO KEEP A DISAGREEMENT FROM BECOMING AN ARGUMENT

Let me share ten tips with you that will help keep a disagreement from turning into an argument which could spell the ruin of your marriage, your business, your partnership, or your dream.

1. *WELCOME THE DISAGREEMENT.* Remember the slogan, "When two partners always agree, one of them is not necessary." If there is some point you haven't thought about be thankful if it is brought to your attention. *Perhaps this disagreement is your opportunity to be corrected before you make a serious mistake.*

This may be an opportunity to impress on your teammates the extent of your emotional maturity. A grumbling rider on a Chicago bus finally got off after scolding the driver in a terrible public scene. As the disagreeable passenger was leaving a voice called out "Just a minute, you left something behind."

"What?" the ruffian demanded.

"A very bad impression," a gentle old lady answered.

On the other hand a disagreement may be an opportunity to leave behind a wonderful impression.

2. *SUSPECT AND DISTRUST YOUR FIRST INSTINCTIVE IMPRESSION.* Our first natural reaction in a disagreeable situation is to be defensive. Be careful. Keep calm and watch out for your first reaction. It may be you at your worst, not your best.

3. *CONTROL YOUR TEMPER.* A friend of mine who enjoys wonderful personnel relations in his shop has a sign hanging in a prominent place where all employees can read it. "You can measure the size of a man by what makes him angry."

4. *GIVE YOUR OPPONENT A CHANCE TO TALK.* Let him finish. LISTEN. Do not resist, defend, or debate. This only raises barriers. Try to build bridges of understanding. Don't build higher barriers of misunderstanding. Continuous interruptions will agitate an already nervous person. It will make an insecure person more defensive and dangerous. Argue and you will further stimulate his imagination to dream up reasons why he is right. Just listen politely.

5. *LOOK FOR AREAS OF AGREEMENT*. When you have heard him out dwell first on the points and areas on which you agree.

6. *BE HONEST*. Look for areas where you can admit error, then tell him so. Apologize for your mistakes. It will help disarm him and reduce his defensiveness.

7. *PROMISE TO THINK OVER AND CAREFULLY STUDY HIS IDEAS*. And mean it. He may be right. It is a lot easier at this stage to agree to think about his points than to move rapidly ahead and find yourself in a position where your opponent can say, "I tried to tell him but he wouldn't even listen."

8. *THANK HIM SINCERELY FOR HIS INTEREST*. Anyone who takes the time to disagree with you is interested in the same things as you. Imagine him as someone who really wants to help and he will turn out to be a friend.

9. *IF YOUR OPPONENT IS A PERSON WHO REALLY BELIEVES IN PRAYER, SUGGEST THAT YOU PRAY TOGETHER*. Ask him to join you in a prayer for divine help and guidance. Pray out loud if you can. At least, pray silently.

10. *THEN, POSTPONE FULLER DISCUSSION TO GIVE BOTH OF YOU TIME TO THINK THROUGH THE PROBLEM*. Suggest that a new meeting be held later that day or the next day when all the facts may be brought to bear.

In preparation for this meeting *ask yourself some hard questions.*

Could my opponent be right? Partly right? Is there truth or merit in his position or argument? Is my reaction one that will relieve the problem or will it just relieve my frustration? Will my reaction drive him further away or draw him closer to me? Will my reaction elevate the estimation good people have of me? Will I win or lose? What price will I have to pay if I win? If I am quiet about it will the disagreement blow over? Is this difficult situation an opportunity for me?

Prepare to *ask your opponent questions.*

Disarming questions—"Do you feel I can help solve this problem?"

Bridge-building questions—"I'd like to help you. Why don't we try to solve this problem together?"

Patience generating questions—"Why don't we take a little more time to think about it?"

Questions that foster understanding—"I am sure you have many good reasons for thinking the way you do. But since I don't see it your way, won't you share them with me?"

Truth-revealing questions—"You seem to be better informed than I. Where and when did you get this information?"

Tolerance-producing questions—"I still can see another side to this. May I share my thoughts on this with you?"

Questions that may point up your opponent's weaknesses and disadvantages—"Do you see any dangers that could arise if we followed your suggestions?"

Questions which put your opponent in your shoes—"What would you do if you were in my position?"

Questions which create an atmosphere for compromise and negotiation—"What, as you see it, are the alternatives?" "Could we ask someone else for an opinion?"

Questions that beg for time—"If what you say is correct we will have to take the time to re-examine our policy (or attitude or position). Let me study over your findings so that we can get together soon to explore various solutions."

Always bear in mind that many of these people who seem to oppose you and are troublesome may become very valuable. It is important to have patience in dealing with them.

Patience is an invaluable tool in dealing with problem people just as it is also extremely valuable in facing many apparently insurmountable barriers.

It is amazing how time performs miracles.

XI

PATIENCE—THE MASTER KEY

Often you can accomplish the seemingly impossible if you don't care how long it takes. We are an impatient race of men. This is the instamatic age. The urge for immediate results can be a dynamic motivational force, but we must learn that mountains are not moved overnight.

Madame Curie made nearly four hundred tedious experiments before she succeeded. The stupendously beautiful temples in Baalbek were built over a period of two hundred years. Many of the magnificent cathedrals in Europe took hundreds of years to complete.

As you face your dream, confront your problem, or offer your prayer, remember that patience is a vital factor in success. It may hold the master key. The U.S. Army Corps of Engineers have this inspiring slogan:

> **The difficult we do immediately—
> the impossible takes a little longer.**

One of the most inspiring accounts of patience I know is that of Dr. Wilhelm De Nejs, who heads the Services for the Blind in Santa Ana, California. Thanks to Dr. De Nejs dozens of sightless people are learning to walk again with their long white canes. They are finding courage to live again—with the encouragement and help of my friend, Wilhelm De Nejs.

"Can you imagine an electrician going totally blind and then learning how to continue his trade and be able to compete with sighted people?" Wilhelm asked me.

"Is that possible?" I replied.

"Anything is possible if a person has enough faith and patience," the doctor answered. He explained how one blind electrician came to the center and was taught to continue his vocation of laying electric wire in new house construction. He was taught how to tell the difference between the black wire and the white wire. There is a difference in the way the wires are coiled in the shipping container. With that tip to start him off, the sightless worker slowly and patiently regained his confidence until today he works as fast and as efficiently as a sighted person.

Dr. De Nejs has inspired hundreds of blind people to begin again. He, himself, has only partial vision.

Out of a difficult personal experience he learned the value of patience. The De Nejses lived in Indonesia and when Sukarno came to power they were forced to flee. Wilhelm's father had been a member of the ruling family of Java and some of Sukarno's associates were determined to destroy all who had royal blood.

"You must leave before they kill you," friends told him. "You and your wife can make it across open water to Singapore, after dark, in a canoe, if you take nothing with you. We will arrange to ship your automobile to Singapore for you."

After arriving safely in Singapore, Wilhelm made plans to get to the Netherlands, where his five children were studying. How was he to do it? All he had was his little car and a small amount of cash.

Invited to address a local Rotary Club meeting about the situation in Indonesia, he also told the members of his plans. "I've decided that we shall drive to Holland in my Tempo Matador auto. I'll try to earn some money for food and gas as we go along. From Holland I hope to go to the United States to learn new methods of helping people who have lost most of their eyesight like I have. I want to help people help themselves."

The audience was deeply moved at this strong statement of faith. After the talk one of the audience shook hands with him warmly, smiling his compliments, as he said, "I am an executive with the Shell Oil Company. I admire your courage."

Reaching into his pocket he pulled out a yellow card and handed it to De Nejs. "Here is a credit card. You can charge all the gas and oil you need on this card and I'll take care of the bill. But," the oil man warned him, "the regular road ends fifty miles outside of town—your trip may not cost me very much."

Heading north out of Singapore, their little car loaded with as many supplies as they could carry, the De Nejses started their journey. It wasn't too long before

Mrs. De Nejs exclaimed to her husband, "Wilhelm, look. There's no more road. Your friend was right."

"We'll use the open areas for a road," her half-blind husband declared. "We've got plenty of time. Let's go."

They bumped along over the fields but before long the wheels of their car began to spin hopelessly in the soggy soil.

"Now what?" his wife asked.

Just then a group of curious native farmers came out of the surrounding hills to investigate the strange sounds the automobile was making as the wheels spun angrily in the stubborn mud.

"We're driving to Holland," shouted Wilhelm, pointing in the general direction of that country and indicating to the visitors the nature of their predicament.

The natives pushed and pulled and slowly moved the car out of the mud up onto a hard elephant trail, wide enough for the little car. Along elephant trails, onto roads when they could find them, the De Nejses moved slowly up the Malay Peninsula. Time and time again they came to rivers with no bridges. De Nejs would test the depth of the water. If he could wade across he would return to drive the car into the shallow water and across the river. But, often, the water was deep. Then he would remove the motor, put it on the roof of the car and he and his wife would push it across. Sometimes, natives attracted by the sight of these two brave foreigners struggling through the jungles would help them build a raft on which they could float the car across.

On they plunged, heading for the famous Stilwell Road, which they hoped would be an easier trip. But rock slides, overgrowth, and disuse had made the road almost impassable. They did what they could, cleaning away debris and underbrush, and pushed bravely on. Finally they reached the Pakistan border and continued their way patiently across East Pakistan, then India. They traveled over the Khyber Pass into Afghanistan, where the nights were freezing.

"We'll have to drain the radiator at night and wait until the water thaws in the morning," Wilhelm explained. Many a night they repeated this procedure.

After passing through Iran and Iraq they reached the border of Syria. Here the guards decided that the De Nejs papers did not meet Syrian requirements and they were denied entrance. It was a bad blow. Was this the end of the journey?

The two determined people sat in their car, silently praying. A stranger, noting their predicament, leaned his head through the open car window. "Wait near here," he said. "Tomorrow, the next day, soon, a sandstorm will come. Then you will be able to drive across the border. No one will see you. And even if they do, they won't chase you. They will not risk their lives—these sandstorms can kill a camel."

So, these two patient people waited in their little car. And waited. And waited. One day a wisp of sand blew gently across the road. The wisp became a drift. First faintly, then stronger, the desert wind mounted until the storm hit with a blinding fury. The border guards retreated into their guardhouse.

"I couldn't see the guardhouse. I couldn't even see ten feet in front of us. I just started the car and drove straight ahead across the Syrian border. No one stopped us. No one cared. I kept driving until I felt we were well inside the country. Then we waited for the storm to die down," De Nejs recalls.

"Where's the road, Wilhelm?" Marianka asked.

"There isn't any. It's lost under the sand."

Then they spotted what would become their road

signs across the desert, the legs of dead camels, caught in the killing storm, which protruded above the sand-buried road. I have seen Wilhelm's remarkable photographs showing the vulture-plucked bones of the camels.

Before they finished crossing the desert their water ran out. For fourteen days they lived virtually without water, taking only a few sips a day from their meager supply. When they finally reached a desert oasis, De Nejs bent over to wash his face, to discover that the water was bitter. So, he drained the dirty but sweet water from the car's radiator and drank that, replacing the radiator water with the bitter water.

Once across the desert they reached Turkey. They crossed the Bosporus and moved into Bulgaria, then on to Yugoslavia. Here they had their first and only accident. On a narrow road De Nejs lost control and the car tipped over into a ditch. "No injuries," he explains laughingly, "just a damaged car."

Seven days later, with repairs made, they were on the road again. The car doors were tied shut with wire, the motor was coughing and missing as they came up to the Austrian Alps. They crossed them and there ahead were the beautiful green hills and valleys of Germany. They came to a town which housed the Tempo Matador automobile factory—the same place where their now battered car had been manufactured three years before. The factory superintendent was so overwhelmed by De Nejs's report, and the photos taken en route, that his car was repaired without charge. Now it was smooth riding into the Netherlands, into the waiting arms of his happy children.

They had made it. In six months, twenty thousand miles, crossing deserts and jungles, across dozens of rivers without bridges, they had finally reached their destination.

What kept them going, mile after mile, month after month? "We had faith in our Lord," De Nejs testifies today, with a radiant face. "We believe deeply that if we had the patience and faith, nothing was impossible."

Somehow we must discover that time can be put to work for us. And with the passing of months and years, we will find solutions to seemingly impossible problems.

I have been both amused and inspired by this story:

The first man said, "I am hungry enough to eat an elephant."

The second man challenged: "How could you eat an elephant?"

The first man answered confidently, "One bite at a time!" An old slogan puts the same truth more succinctly:

> **"Inch by inch anything's a cinch!"**

The people who win in life are the people who have harnessed the power of patience. You can move a mountain, Christ said—but He didn't say how long it would take.

A friend of mine was in her mid-seventies when she suffered an almost fatal heart attack. There was little hope that she could recover. Great prayer went forth. She recovered. But the doctor advised that her hopes for living more than a few months were very dim. Her only hope was to lose about sixty pounds of excess weight. The suggestion seemed impossible. "Why, all I will have to do is lose a pound a week and in about a year it will be gone," she thought. She made a plan with her doctor. She reduced. Victoriously! And she has enjoyed five wonderful years of outgoing health since that day.

A young man lost his wife and daughter through divorce. The husband was brokenhearted when he came to our office. We prayed deeply. "At least I must get custody of my daughter," the wonderful father said anxiously. "But everyone tells me that it is impossible for a father to win custody over daughters in our courts." Nothing is impossible, I reminded my close friend. It took him two years, but he won permanent custody of his beautiful daughter. Every day this father would wash, iron, do the housework, being a mother and father to this lovely little girl, working nights to earn his living. All the while he taught Sunday-school classes each week in his church. Then God brought to his life one of the finest examples of Christian womanhood I have ever met. She was a wonderful widow. They married. And she could not be surpassed as a wife and a mother to this wonderful man and his daughter. His name? Norman Miner. His job? Manager of the Orange Drive-In Theater for five years while I preached from the snack bar roof top. "Reverend, I wasn't a Christian the first two years you preached out there. Then I wondered what you were talking about. I listened secretly to an overflow speaker in my private office. How I thank God I was converted to a life of faith in God. He has helped me through the toughest problem any man can face."

All in all, it took four years for Norm Miner's prayers to be answered. I have often thought how tragic it would have been if, lacking patience, he had given up somewhere in those dark days.

There is almost no problem that patience cannot solve.

There is almost no dream that patience cannot push to victory.

Take the case of this young boy. He was having arguments with his dad. They fought. For months they did not talk. Dad went to work. Son went to school. Then he decided to drop out of school and join the army. There was a war going on, overseas as well as in his own heart and home. The day came for him to leave. As he stood at the door with his suitcase, he heard a sound behind him. Turning, he saw his father standing there. Without speaking, this powerful hulk of a man just looked at his son. The middle-aged eyes flooded with tears as he ran to his grown-up boy and hugged him. Tough cheeks slid together through hot tears. No words were spoken. Then the boy left for military service. The bus windows were steamed up. Or was it a mist in his young eyes? One thing was clear. In this young man's mind was the thought, "My dad loved me all along and I didn't know it." Years passed. The toughened soldier came home. What job could a school dropout get? Well, he could drive a truck. He enjoyed his new job. For more years than he likes to count, he delivered pies. Then an inspiration came. Christ came into his life. And when Christ comes in, big thinking comes in. "I'd like to help people get their tangled lives straightened out," he thought. "I'd like to be a psychologist. I will be a psychologist! I don't care how long it takes. I am going to become a psychologist." Today, years later, that man, Dr. Mead, is a practicing counselor helping hundreds of people through their difficulties.

Are you at a difficult time in your life? Make no negative, destructive decisions. Be patient. Know that time can perform miracles.

Truly, patience is one of the master keys that leads to success.

You will need patience if you wish to succeed in facing problems.

You will need patience if you wish to succeed in making your dreams come true.

And you will need patience if you hope to see answers to your prayers.

Possibility thinkers are people who have come to believe deeply in a Living God who hears and answers prayer.

God answers prayers in several ways:

1. He gives us exactly what we ask for, right away.
2. He gives us what we ask for—weeks, months, sometimes years later.
3. He gives us not what we asked for, but what we really wanted—even though we may not know what that is.
4. He gives us not what we asked for, nor what we really wanted, but what was best.

I have had absolutely miraculous answers to prayer in my personal life. I have already told of how my plan for a walk-in drive-in church succeeded. When I was dreaming of the new church, I prayed that God would give us a chance to buy a piece of property that I was sure was the perfect place to build our dream church. It was a beautiful walnut grove. In my judgment, it was the ideal location near the heart of the city of Garden Grove. It was not for sale, but I was confident that if I would only pray God would make it available.

One Sunday afternoon I walked alone into the ten acres of trees and opened my Bible to the text "Ask whatever you will and it will be given you." I started to pray (standing up because I was wearing my best suit). I suddenly thought that if I was more concerned about dust on my pants than getting God to help me, my thinking was wrong. So I knelt in the dirt, put my finger on the Bible verse, and prayed, "Dear God. Please let this owner agree to sell us this property." I arose. I left—confident that we would purchase this land. Well, we failed. The owner absolutely refused to sell—even though we offered twelve thousand dollars an acre.

Months later we were offered, and we bought, our present property for only $6600 an acre. "Not as central a location—way on the east edge of Garden Grove, that's the only thing wrong with it," one of my friends observed. I was inclined to agree. Then came the unfolding of the state's freeway plans and we found that our "in-the-sticks ten acres" was at a spot where three freeways would join. We found ourselves not in the center of a city of 100,000 people, but at the highway hub in the center of a county of over one million people! God—in time—answered our prayers not as we asked, but in a much better way.

I remembered then that God has never promised to give us exactly what we ask for WHEN we ask for it. Someone said:

> **"God's delays are not God's denials."**

How can we get the patience we need to win? By trusting God to guide us to the right place, at the right time, in the right way.

GOD'S TIMING IS MUCH BETTER THAN OURS

Are we moving too fast? Or are we moving too slowly? Should we plunge ahead—or wait? What decision maker, facing opportunities, has not raised this question? For timing is all-important in every venture of life. If God is your partner, He will help you time things wisely.

Chances are God will time things out in such a way

that when He answers your prayer, He will be answering many prayers. God is big. So big that when He answers one prayer, He answers many prayers.

Here is my witness. Here is what happened to me. While I prayed for our dream to be fulfilled, many other people in far-off places, with totally different dreams, were also praying—totally different prayers.

Halfway around the world a young refugee in Indonesia, named Maurice Wiggers, was praying that somehow, someway, he might be able to come to the United States of America and find a job and a life in this land of the free. Half a world away, in Singapore, a great missionary, Henry Poppen, preparing for retirement, was praying that upon his return to America some opportunity would let him continue to serve God.

In Canada a young Dutch immigrant, Peter De-Graaf, was praying for a chance to come to the United States with an opportunity to begin a business of his own.

Half a continent away, a young minister, Harold Leestma, was praying for greater opportunities to reach more lives for Jesus Christ in his one lifetime.

And in Holland, Michigan, Reverend Kenneth Van Wyk was specializing in the study of youth and education problems and praying for guidance.

While Henry Poppen was praying in Singapore, and Maurice Wiggers in praying in Indonesia, and Peter DeGraaf was praying in Canada, and Harold Leestma was praying in Indiana, and Kenneth Van Wyk was praying in Holland, Michigan, I was impatiently praying in Garden Grove, California. Why didn't God answer my prayer and make it possible for us to buy the ten-acre walnut grove so we could build our great dream?

With the passing of years, I can see that God was

timing everything in such a way that when He answered my prayer, He would be answering many prayers—all in one masterful stroke! For today Maurice Wiggers has come from Indonesia to the United States and is the custodian of Garden Grove Community Walk-In Drive-In Church. This church is an answer to his prayer. Dr. Henry Poppen on his return to America became our Minister of Visitation. This church is an answer to his Singapore prayer. Kenneth Van Wyk is now our Minister of Youth and Education. This church is an answer to his Michigan prayer. Harold Leestma is our Minister of Evangelism. This church is an answer to his prayer in Indiana. Peter DeGraaf is our church gardener. This church is an answer to his prayer in Canada. God timed things so that many prayers were answered in one beautiful development. Be patient; God is working everything out. At the right time and in the right way everything will evolve beautifully.

Don't try to rush God.

Mountains don't move overnight.

Give God time to work His miracles.

I have seen God dissolve resentments,
    resolve frustrations,
    fill lonely hearts with new love,
    and wash away hurts like a new wave
    washes away scars on sand
    scratched by children's sticks.

God can get you out of a rut,
    onto a new road,
    and over the mountain that seemed impassable,
    if you will be patient.

I have seen God turn juvenile delinquents into great men,
    criminals into good citizens,
    alcoholics into church elders.

She was a beautiful wife of an alcoholic husband. Let's call him Jim Smith. She poured out the story of her husband's fifteen years of horrible drinking. "He's gone now, Reverend. He left a week ago. I have no idea where he is. But I can't—I just can't stand it any longer."

"Let's pray," I offered. "Dear God, wherever Jim is right now, you touch him, come into his mind in the form of a redeeming powerful idea. Save him." It was all I could do. Unknown to us, at that very moment Jim was lying in a cheap hotel in Chicago. A strange Power came over him. Let him tell his story. Here is what he wrote in a letter I received ten days later:

Dear Reverend:

I suppose that it is odd that you should receive a letter from a troubled mind from so far away, however I thought that I would take this opportunity to talk with you for awhile.

I am an alcoholic. My crimes while drunk fall short of many moral standards, to say the least. I have cheated, stolen, lied, and short of murder or rape, I have done everything wrong.

I found my God, my real One, the One that I didn't think could forgive me for some of these most terrible deeds.

It came about in this manner. I asked myself this question, "If a man came to me, and laid the whole mess of his life before me to hear and weigh, could I, Jim Smith, forgive him if he were truly sorry?"

Yes, Reverend, I could! This was my answer to this question. So then came the next question. "If I could do this, then who on earth am I to doubt that my God could not forgive me?"

My own guilt complex was so intensified that I had shut Him out completely. For the first time in my life I got on my knees and asked Him to help me. There weren't any bright lights, no big booms and no loud "Yes, my son, you are forgiven."

ᶠ But there was a slow creeping pringly feeling up and down the whole of me. This then was my answer—my inner self crying in the dark.

I had been drunk for seven days and nights. Now I have been sober for seven days and nights. I called my wife. She said she talked with you. I have no idea what was said between you, but I do know that this Great Force put us together again. And in a day or so, I shall have made enough money to fly home to my wife and three sons.

I shall work very hard to win their love and trust back, for it will not ever be again like it was if I can get on my knees and ask my real Father to forgive me.

Respectfully yours,

Jim Smith

So God performed the miracle. Today I can report that Jim's life is miraculously changed.

AGAIN AND AGAIN THE MAN WHO WINS IS THE MAN WHO NEVER FORGETS THAT

after the night comes a new day,
after the winter another spring,
after the storm a sun-drenched earth,
after sin comes forgiveness,
after defeat another chance.

Some time ago a dynamic businessman whom I had not seen for many years came into my office. "How good to see you again! How are things going with you?" I asked. "Very well now, thank you, Reverend," he said with a spark in his eyes. "It took me a while to bounce back after my reversals, but I'm on top of things again." Puzzled, I asked him, "What do you mean, reversals?" Then he told me his story. An unscrupulous partner in a business venture mismanaged company funds, which plunged his business into an insolvent condition. Here is how he tells his story:

I tried to stall creditors off, promising that somehow, someway, I would repay everyone with interest. I begged for time. All of them trusted me except one. It was this one untrusting and high-pressuring creditor that forced me into a situation where my only recourse was bankruptcy. It was a terribly humiliating experience.

I drove to the court in Long Beach, California, and when I left that court, I was not even permitted to drive my own car home! It had become the property of the court. I was never so embarrassed in my life as I was when I went out of court, empty-handed, without the keys to my car. I had to hitchhike back to Garden Grove. I stood on Seventh Street in Long Beach trying to thumb a ride home. I hoped I would not be seen by anybody who knew me. I thought to myself, "What will I tell people if they ask why I am hitchhiking?" Just then a truck stopped and offered me a lift. The driver sensed that I was discouraged and tried to make happy talk. But I am afraid I was not a very enthusiastic conversationalist. I felt defeated and beaten.

When I arrived home, I realized that I had lost everything. I was in my mid-fifties. What kind of a future did I have? It looked pretty black. Then I began to pray to God for help and for strength. In my time of prayer, it seemed like I heard a bell ring in my mind. I imagined myself a fighter in a boxing ring, knocked down and for a moment knocked out, only to be revived by the ringing of a bell. Of course. I had only lost one round! This was not the end of the fight. I would pull myself to my knees, crawl back to my corner, have my face washed with cold water, and come out from the corner of the ring fighting again! I wasn't finished until I decided to give up. And I was not going to give up.

I would be patient. I would remain calm. I would wait and look for new opportunities. Surely they would come. I wasn't finished. Not yet!

Well, that patience rescued an otherwise defeated man from fatal pessimism and moved him into a mood of unconquerable optimism. In this frame of mind enthusiasm returned. No wonder he found another job. Dedicated and enthusiastic people can find employment. He managed to save enough money to get back on his feet. He soon owned another car, and as I discovered in the course of conversation, he had just been offered the job of national field manager of a great industrial organization at a salary of fifty thousand dollars a year. He repaid in full the debts that were legally erased by the bankruptcy court.

Remember:

> **You're not defeated**
> **until you lose your patience.**

XII

WHEN IT LOOKS LIKE YOU'RE FINISHED—HOLD ON!

WHEN ALL THE MONEY IN THE WORLD, ALL THE MANPOWER ON PLANET EARTH, AND ALL OF TIME IN ETERNITY SEEMS USELESS in the face of your problem—what then?

When the way ahead looks terribly dark, the impossibility thinker will pity himself, panic inside, pack up, and quit. Perhaps with a bottle or a box of pills.

But the POSSIBILITY THINKER somehow manages to keep hoping in hope.

A Jew, one of many hiding from Hitler, once knew such a dark time. We know neither his name nor his face, but we know about his faith. For scrawled on the basement walls of a German house are these courageous words:

> I believe in the sun even when it is not shining,
> I believe in love even when I do not feel it.
> I believe in God, even when He is silent.

When the situation looks hopeless, keep hoping. When everything looks impossible, refuse to accept defeat.

I learned this lesson the night I outraced the tornado. I was back home in Iowa only one week after my first year in college. Throughout the afternoon my Dad and I could hear an awesome roar that sounded high in the darkened western sky. It was an eerie sound—like many freight trains rumbling above the clouds. "Sounds like we're in for a hailstorm," Dad predicted. He was worried about his prize roses. In a desperate attempt to protect them, we rounded up empty pails and wooden boxes to cover every treasured bush. It was six o'clock now. We had finished our evening meal in haste. From the vantage point of our front lawn we could see more than a mile across the rolling farm land. The sun was lost now, seemingly swallowed by the black monstrous storm that was prowling the western sky. Slowly, with an alarming stillness, like a creeping tiger crawling up on a sleeping prey, the storm crept closer. Gusts of hot wind blew dry dust on the country road. The old box elder began bending before the mounting winds. Out in the pasture I could hear a cow bellow frantically, calling her little calf to come to her side for safety. I could see my riding horse standing in the green pasture. He seemed to sense impending disaster. He cut a commanding picture, standing erect, with his head held high; his graceful neck arched; his tail, lifted slightly, blowing wildly in the wind; his ears pricking the air for sounds of danger.

Suddenly a black lump, about the size of the sun, bulged out of the black sky. In an instant it telescoped into a long gray funnel snaking its way down to the ground. For a moment it hung suspended like a slithering serpent about to strike a death sting on helpless victims below. Dad called Mom: "It's a tornado, Jennie!"

I asked excitedly, "Are you sure it's a real tornado, Dad?" My first emotion was delightful excitement. This would be something to tell the fellows when I'd return to Hope College in the fall. The funnel seemed so small I couldn't imagine the fury that could be unleashed from such a funny cloud.

"Call Mother, son, and tell her to take whatever she can grab and come to the car. We've got to get out of here—right away!"

A moment later we were driving crazily down the road. We lived on the east end of a dead-end road and had to drive a mile west, directly into the path of the oncoming tornado to reach a side road that would head south and away from the path of the storm. We made it. Two miles south, we parked our car on the crest of the hill and watched the wicked twister spend its killing power. As quickly and quietly as it had dropped, it lifted and disappeared. It was all over. The storm was gone. The air was deathly still, but the danger was past. Gentle raindrops now began to fall. The tail end of the dark sky dropped a soothing shower of cool rain, as if heaven was pouring a soothing balm on fresh wounds.

We could go home now. (Oh, God, will we find our house?) We reached the crossroads, only to find a long line of cars. Curious sight-seers, sensing that something terrible had happened, already were gathering. They were looking at the complete destruction of a neighboring farm. Wondering if our house had been spared, we drove down the lonely road that led to our secluded farm. Wires from broken telephone poles crisscrossed the road. We came to the base of the hill that hid the view of our house. We could always see the peak of our barn rise above the hill. But not now. We knew before we went over the hill that our barn was gone. Now we were on the top of the hill. We saw it. Everything was gone. Where only a half hour before there were nine buildings, freshly painted, now there were none. Where there was life, there was the silence of death. It was all gone. It was all dead. We were dazed; our brains reeled. Only white foundations remained, lying on a clean patch of black ground. There was no debris. Everything had simply been sucked up and carried away. A dead pig was lying in the driveway. Three little pigs, still living, sucked the breasts of their dead mother. We could hear the sickening moan of dying cattle, the hiss of gas escaping from a portable tank of butane used to provide fuel for our stove. Then I saw my riding horse —lying dead with a fourteen-foot-long two-by-four piercing his belly.

Stunned, we sat in our car. My father was past sixty and had worked hard for twenty-six years to try to win this farm. The mortgage was about due. This seemed to kill all chances of ever saving the place from the creditors. I looked at my dad, sitting horror-eyed in the front seat—my dad, white-haired, underweight from overwork, hands blue, desperately gripping the steering wheel. Suddenly these calloused hands with bulging blood vessels began hitting the steering wheel of the car, and Dad cried, "It's all gone! Jennie! Jennie, it's all gone! Twenty-six years, Jennie, and it's all gone

in ten minutes." Dad got out of the car, ordering us to
wait. We could see him walking with his cane around
the clean-swept, tornado-vacuumed farmyard. We
found out later that our house had been dropped in
one smashed piece a half mile out in the pasture. We
had a little sign in the kitchen—one of these little
molded plaster mottos that you hang on the wall. It
was a simple verse that said, "Keep looking to Jesus."
My dad found and carried to the car the top broken
half that said simply: "Keep looking. . . ." Well, this
was God's message to Dad—Keep looking! Keep looking!

Don't quit now. Don't sell out. Dig in and hold on.
And he did! People thought that my dad was finished,
but he was not. He was not finished because he would
not give up. He had faith with hanging-on power!
There's one ingredient that mountain-moving faith,
miracle-generating faith, earth-shaking faith, problem-
solving faith, situation-changing faith must have, and
that ingredient is HOLDING power. So Dad didn't quit.

Two weeks later we found in a nearby town an old
house that was being torn down. A section of it was
still left for sale for fifty dollars. So we bought this
remnant and took it apart, piece by piece. We saved
every nail. We saved every shingle. And from these
pieces we built a new little house on the old home
farm! Piece by piece additional farm buildings were
built. Nine farms were demolished in that tornado but
my father was the only farmer to rebuild a completely
demolished farm. A few years later prices rose sharply.
Farm products prospered. Within five years the mortgage was paid off. My father died a successful man!
"No man having put his hand to the plow and looking
back is fit for the kingdom of God."

Somebody said:

> **"Great people are just ordinary people
> with an extraordinary amount
> of determination."**

Most people who succeed in the face of seemingly impossible conditions are people who simply don't know how to quit.

When unexpected damage wreaks havoc with your dreams, then what? Never dwell on what you have lost. If you do, you will be discouraged and defeated. Look not at what you have lost but at what you have left.

In northwest Iowa lives Walter Greving, a handsome young man who suffered a severe attack of polio. When the disease left him he took stock of the permanent damage. Chest muscles were paralyzed. He would have to spend the rest of his life in an artificial respirator. Arms, legs, hands, shoulders, all were permanently paralyzed. But he could see, think, hear, talk —and he had the use of a single, solitary finger.

Instead of dwelling on what he lost he began to think, "What can I do with what I have left?" He wondered: "What can I do with one finger?"

I was in his room and it was one of the great inspirations of my life. It is incredible what he is able to do with one finger. With one finger he can press a button! And that opens up an almost unlimited assortment of possibilities. A button begins a tape recorder, enabling him to dictate the encouraging letters he sends around the world. A tape recorder, radio, TV, hi-fi, a book "pager" that flips pages of a book he is reading—all are electrically operated and move into action at the press of his one finger!

"I was never happier before polio than I am today. I never really started to live until I got into the iron lung. I learned to think differently," he told me as we visited. Of course, he's a POSSIBILITY THINKER. I have never met a happier man in my life. He is the most popular cheer spreader, gloom chaser, hope builder, joy generator, in the city of Sheldon, Iowa.

A friend of mine told me about his visit to a leprosarium in Japan. Many of the patients who had already lost their eyesight were learning to read by the Braille system. One blind leper tried to learn to read by the Braille system only to find that the deterioration caused by the disease left his fingers so insensitive that he was unable to feel the raised lettering. Give up? Of course not. He tried using his toes! But here, too, the feeling was lacking. What did he have left? Nothing? Something? Of course! He remembered that he had one sensitive part of his body left that might serve him. He tried. It worked! Today he reads his Braille Bible. How? With his tongue!

For three years Reverend Martin Neimoller survived the horrors of Dachau—the smells of burning human flesh and the sights of walking dead men. For three years this German pastor who dared to defy Adolf Hitler was kept in solitary confinement in the world's worst concentration camp.

"How could you stand it without losing your sanity?" an interviewer asked Pastor Neimoller years later over a Chicago radio station. "*A man doesn't realize how much he can stand until he is put to the test,*" Neimoller answered confidently, continuing, "you can stand far more than you think you can. You are much stronger than you think you are . . . *if God is dwelling in your life.*"

William James was the first man to tell us that we have several layers of fatigue. Pass the first layer and suddenly, like an exhausted runner receiving a second wind, the worn-out emotions are revived by a new and amazing source of revitalizing power stronger and more dynamic than the first supply. When it looks like you're finished—hang on!

A. J. Cronin described the turning point of his career in an article in *Reader's Digest*. He was a successful doctor until a serious illness forced him to take a six months' rest in the Scottish Highlands. Here a great idea slashed into his mind. "By heavens," he said, "this is my opportunity. Gastric ulcer or no gastric ulcer, I'll write a novel." He went to the town store, bought paper and pencil, and sat down to write a novel. For three hours he sat at his paper waiting in vain for an inspiration. He decided at lunch it was a silly idea. But he recalled the advice of a schoolteacher who once said, "Get it down—if it stops in your head it will be nothing. Get it down." For three months he labored, wrote, rewrote, until halfway through the novel a sense of futility haunted his thinking. "Why am I wearing myself out with this task for which I am unequipped?" he asked himself. "What's the use of it? I ought to be resting." It was a bunch of nonsense, he concluded. No one would ever read it. He threw the manuscript into the ash can and walked out into the drizzling rain.

At the loch shore he met old Angus, the farmer, patiently digging in the ditch along his little boggy patch of ground. Cronin told his country friend that he had thrown his book away. He was giving up. He simply didn't have the talent, training, or touch needed to be an author. "No doubt you're the one that's right, Doctor, and I'm the one that's wrong," old Angus said. "But my father ditched this bog all my days and I've never made a pasture, but pasture or no pasture, I can't help but dig. For my father knew and I know that if you only dig enough, a pasture can be made here." A new spurt of self-esteem and determination swept through the young doctor's soul. He walked back to the ash can, rescued the soggy manuscript, dried it in the kitchen oven, and went back to work. Some weeks later he finished his task, mailed the book to a publisher and forgot about it. That novel was *Hatter's Castle*. It was dramatized, and translated into nineteen languages, and some three million copies have been sold.

God alone knows how many good books have been burned, how many inspiring ideas have been cast into the wastebasket, how many great projects, programs, and marriages have been discarded by their creators who quit just before the miracle was about to happen.

There come times in the lives of most people when it seems utterly crazy to keep going. When all of common sense seems to shout out, telling you to "Get wise, you're finished! Lay down the sword," be careful. This is the moment of ultimate decision. During that time when the vice president, treasurer, and secretary of my church had resigned, I, too, might have quit. I didn't. I found hanging-on power in words that I had learned years before from my grandfather.

He was an immigrant from the Netherlands who pioneered in the unspoiled Iowa plains. In this land of the Sioux Indians he bought a plow and broke the virgin prairie. The trick, of course, was to plow a straight furrow when there were no boundaries. Here's how he did it.

He walked to the top of the hill, drove a stake. On the stake he tied a red handkerchief. He walked back down the hill and jabbed the sharp tip of the plow into the grass-covered prairie, fixed his eye on the red flag waving in the wind, and whipped his oxen with a loud "Haaaigh!" That's how he plowed his first furrow. "Never take your eye off the flag," he used to tell the late-arriving pioneers. "Once you have hit dirt, and have started for the flag, don't look back. You may slip, you may stumble, you may get tired, and you may have to sit down, but whatever you do, DON'T LOOK BACK OR YOU WILL PLOW A CROOKED FURROW."

Then my grandfather liked to quote the powerful Bible verse: "No man having put his hand to the plow and looking back is fit for the kingdom of God." Don't look back. Don't accept failure. Don't accept defeat. One prominent American businessman has succeeded and failed, succeeded and failed again, and is once more a success. How is he able to come back? The reason was revealed by an intimate who said, "Bill just doesn't know when he is finished. So he hangs in there when by all estimates he should be done for. Something always seems to happen while he is hanging on half-dead and he comes out of it."

In Sacred Heart, Minnesota, there is a beautiful nursery where row on row of prize-winning trees and shrubs are raised and shipped to all parts of the Midwest. The successful owner is a man by the name of Clarence Flagstad. He is a success because he would not accept defeat. It was at the beginning of the Second World War. Together with his father and his brother the family worked to eke out enough to make the mortgage payments. Then the war came. His brother was drafted. Clarence and his dad simply worked harder, hoping to produce more to meet the mounting costs that war brought to most materials. Then the tragic news came. The oldest son had been killed. He would never return to the Minnesota farm. "We'll keep going, Dad. It's what my brother would want us to do," Clarence said. So they held on. Then Clarence's father died. It was the hardest of all blows to the young fellow. He was left alone now. And the pressures from the high-powered financial institution in Chicago for settlements on delinquent mortgage payments became almost more than the lonely young man could endure. Then came the final notice. The letter from Chicago was firm and final: the mortgage was going to be foreclosed. Clarence prayed. "I can't lose this farm. I just can't. What would my dad say? What would my brother say? I'll go to Chicago and talk to them." It was a crazy idea. The processors would be attacking his property before he could reach the big city. Moreover, he didn't have the money for a bus ticket. But he remembered seeing hobos riding on trains. Why not? Late that night he threw his lanky frame on the back of an old caboose just before the slow freight train loaded with cattle pulled out of the little Minnesota town headed for Chicago.

"I prayed deep prayers on that cattle train," he said. "Please, God, help me find the people when I get to Chicago." He found the skyscraping office building, the biggest structure he had ever seen in his life. "I want to see the president of the company," he insisted to the private secretary. When he refused to leave, the secretary spoke to the company head, who happened to be a fine Christian. "Let him come in," the president offered. Clarence later described the meeting: "Why, that big fellow was as nice as pie to me. He said, 'Clarence, we don't want your farm. We only want our money back with interest. That's our business. Now let's sit down and see how we can work this out so you can get that farm paid for.' " So Clarence Flagstad went home not only with a refinancing package fitted to his needs but with new faith that it pays to hang on when by all odds you should be giving up.

Few figures in American history demonstrated this hang-on power more forcefully than did Theodore Roosevelt. When Russia and Japan couldn't settle their differences, Teddy Roosevelt got their representatives over here and, as one Russian said, "he hammered at us with a fist of steel until he starved us into solving our problem." About that time, the Briton John Morley visited America and went back to England, to declare: "I saw two tremendous forces of nature while I was in the New World—one was the Niagara Falls and the other was the President of the United States, Teddy Roosevelt. And I'm not sure which was the more wonderful."

It reminds us of Winston Churchill's commentary on one of his great generals in North Africa. Churchill, describing the general, said, "He is an iron peg anchored in frozen ground—immovable." Champions are people that have great holding power.

While Abe Lincoln was wondering whether or not he should run for a national office, the Missouri Compromise was tragically repealed. The year was 1854. Bungling by some of our less successful Presidents led to the repeal of this slavery-discouraging resolution. Now the rest of the states formed from the slave-practicing Louisiana Purchase territory would join the United States of America and slavery would be encouraged and continued by the federal government! It was at that point that Abe Lincoln showed his great moral strength: "I know that there is a God and that He hates injustice and slavery. I see a storm coming and I know His hand is in it. If He has a place for me, and I think He has, I believe I am ready." So Lincoln put his hand on the plow . . . and the storm fell! And Lincoln found himself President of the United States with Southern states seceding and threatening to secede. He could see this new Union falling apart. There were those who said, "Let the South go. Good riddance to bad rubbish." But Mr. Lincoln's response was contained in six holding-power words: "Hold firm as chains of steel." Result? CIVIL WAR! FIRE! But the salvation of the Union, and the beginning of the end of slavery.

In the battle of life it is the man with holding-power faith who wins.

"I shall return," General MacArthur said when he was pushed from Corregidor. And he did. Many a time in my life when I have needed holding power, I have seen in my mind's eye the famous photograph of MacArthur, open shirt, rumpled hat, corncob pipe, chin out, arms swinging as he waded with powerful stride through foaming waves up the beach to retake the island. He was returning!

In a tough spot right now? You may be on the very edge of winning. Remember what MacArthur said when his forces in Korea were suffering setbacks until they were backed up against the sea?

Someone asked the general what he thought of the desperate situation and he replied with strong voice, "I have never been more confident of victory than I am today." And he was so right. The tide suddenly turned. And he surged ahead and on to victory!

> Great men are ordinary people who
> just will not give up hope.
> And what is Hope?
> It is

Holding On, Praying Expectantly

Years later, people look back upon their darkest day and say—as Churchill said of London's war years— "This was our finest hour."

XIII

MOUNTAIN-MOVING FAITH—HERE'S HOW IT WORKS

NOW   You have seen how possibility thinkers have
made their dreams come true,
turned troubles into personal victories, and
made their lives an inspiration to those around
them.

NOW   You can transform your life and your future—if
You will discover and dispatch the power of
mountain-moving faith to your life situation.

YOU CAN ACCOMPLISH WHAT SEEMS AT THIS MOMENT TO BE AN IMPOSSIBILITY IF YOU WILL TAKE THE EIGHT STEPS OF MOUNTAIN-MOVING FAITH.

"If you have faith as a grain of mustard seed you can say to this mountain: move! And it will move! And nothing will be impossible to you!"

There are many people who claim to live by faith but remain low achievers. We all know individuals who claim to exercise real faith yet they accomplish little or nothing. What's wrong? Frequently failure is the result of a too-shallow faith.

I walk to the beach and I see people cautiously putting their toes in the edge of the ocean. They splash around ankle-deep, come back to lie down in the sun, and go home claiming they have been swimming.

There are others who wade waist-deep in the water before they turn back to lie on the warm sand.

Then there is the real venturer who moves steadily deeper until the water reaches his shoulders and he begins to swim. He has moved to the deeper level and can honestly claim that he has been swimming.

Mountain-moving faith is not merely touching your toes in the water. Mountain-moving faith is faith that dares to step into deep water.

LOOK NOW AT THE EIGHT STEPS OF MOUNTAIN-MOVING FAITH

STEP 1. DREAMING. This is faith taking the first cautious step. Mountain-moving faith begins with a dream. Unquestionably the greatest power in the world is the power of a creative idea. All success begins with a dream. One of America's great teachers was Thomas S. Kelly. The secret of his effective life, according to Rufus Jones, goes back to a single moment in Kelly's freshman year at college when he had a dream—and he said, "I'm going to make my life a miracle!" Someone said, "There are no great men: only great ideas." Indeed, you can often measure the size of a man by the size of his dreams.

Faith begins with an act of imagining. "If you don't have a dream, how can dreams come true?" Begin now by using this God power within yourself to paint a picture of what you would like to accomplish.

Reject all impossibility thoughts, all "handicapped concepts," and all disadvantage complexes. Imagine yourself as a friend of the mighty, a partner of the wealthy, and a co-worker with God. Faith begins with a dream. But faith must move to deeper levels before success will be realized.

STEP 2. DESIRING. Faith in deeper water is wanting something so badly that someday, somehow, somewhere, sometime, you know you shall have it. More faith is shattered by lack of desire than by real doubt.

No man will ever believe that he can move a mountain unless he really wants that mountain to move. Almost anything can be accomplished by the person who really wants to succeed. The old adage is so true: If there's a will, there's a way.

> We believe what we want to believe!
> Believing is wanting!

Apply this definition of faith to your project and your dreams. To begin with, you must know what you want. Not a few people fail because they have neglected to visualize in detail what they were trying to achieve. If you have a confused and muddled picture of what you are going after, do not be surprised if you fail. Therefore, an early step in mountain-moving faith is forming a detailed mental picture of your dream.

As the sharp details of your dream come into clear mental focus, you will find your enthusiasm mounting to an ever higher pitch.

If you want your dream badly enough, you will plan, organize, reorganize, and work, until you get what you want. Great desire marshals great determination. And success awaits the man who will "never say never." You never really fail until you stop wanting. Faith is wanting something with all your heart!

After you know what you want, you must censor these desires. The moral questions must be raised at this point: "Is this right? Would God want this? Can I ask God to be my partner in this venture?" Faith builds strong muscles when it gets a "Yes" answer to these all-important questions.

STEP 3. DARING. Doubt is frequently a lack of courage. Fear of embarrassment, along with fear of involvement, or fear of personal self-sacrifice, is enough to keep many a person from wanting to make a commitment of faith to an idea, a dream, a project, or a cause. With God on your side you will dare to run risks!

Mountain-moving faith is not merely dreaming and desiring; it is daring to risk failure. For faith is making a decision with no guarantee of success. If success is certain, then a venture is no longer an act of faith. Faith without risk is a contradiction. Faith is taking a chance on something before you can be sure how everything will finally work out. Remember:

EVERY TIME YOU MAKE A CHOICE YOU TAKE A CHANCE

Even indecision is a decision. And even if you decide to do nothing you run the risk of failing to attempt what might have become a marvelous miracle. Don't forget: "The saddest words of tongue or pen are these—it might have been."

If we had not built our walk-in drive-in church I would have been haunted all my life by the thought that it might have been one of the greatest successes of my life. I was more fearful of bypassing a rare and rich opportunity than I was of making a costly and foolish mistake.

The truth is, many people fail and never know it. They go through life without a single apparent setback. They never suffer embarrassment or reversals.

They think they are successful. But the truth is, they fail because they neglected to spot and develop the once-in-a-lifetime opportunity. They are failures but do not know it.

Faith is daring to risk disappointment. POSSIBILITY THINKERS have cast the fear of personal disappointment from their thinking! How many people never enter a contest, never compete in the games, never commit their lives to something that has the prospect of greatness, for fear of losing?

"If you never try, you will never lose." How my heart sank when I heard that depressing and erroneous statement by an otherwise intelligent young man. "It just is not true. You can lose what you could have had," I told him.

One of the tragedies of life is that too many people deliberately set their goals too low, to reduce the possibility of disappointment. Obviously, our goals must be realistic, but high enough so that success can be termed a miracle. Not a few people claim to be a success because they've reached every goal in life. The truth is, they are really failures because their goals were deceptively low.

On the other hand, many people have been proclaimed failures because they never achieved their highest goal, simply because their goal was too high. They did not reach their goal, but they did reach their maximum potential. And that's being a success! Success is not necessarily reaching your goal, but success is reaching your maximum possibility in the light of the opportunities that came your way.

Faith is daring to risk public criticism. The truth is that every pioneer project is criticized by negative people. Now, public opinion is not to be totally disregarded, but it must be put in its proper place. We should remember that we must live with some people part of our life; we must live with a few people most of our life; but we must live with ourselves all of our life; and we must live with God forever! Ask these decision-making questions in this order: (1) What does God think? (2) What do you, in your own heart, think? (3) What do your wise friends think? (4) What would the public think? Public opinion is the last question to be asked—not the first! The POSSIBILITY THINKER then makes his decision, knowing that if need be he will remold a hesitant or hostile public opinion.

Faith is daring to risk imperfection. "If it can't be a best seller, I won't publish it," I once thought. Until this idea struck me:

> **Better to do something imperfectly
> than to do nothing perfectly!**

The tragic truth is that much of our efforts would be overwhelmingly successful if we dared to run the risk of mediocrity. What we judge to be mediocre may be judged by others to be excellent. Norman Vincent Peale worked long and hard on his first manuscript. Finally, convinced in his own mind that it was not good enough, he threw it in a wastebasket. Fortunately, it was picked out of the basket, sent to the publishers, and appeared in the bookstores of the country under the title *A Guide to Confident Living*. It has sold more than a million copies.

Faith is daring to be a chance-taker. Do you know what POSSIBILITY THINKERS fear more than failure? It is the fear of becoming stale, stagnant, and tired. It is the fear of the adventure-stifling, courage-strangulating inclination to "play it safe."

> Give us now and then a man
> And life will crown him king,
> Who dares to face the consequence
> Just to risk the thing!

Here's how success will work for you:

Chance-taking generates excitement. Excitement generates enthusiasm. Enthusiasm generates energy. You have a success cycle going.

You are suddenly catapulted into the spotlight. The attention is never on the comfortable spectator, but on the energetic chance-taker in the center ring. And the bigger the gamble, the bigger the crowd of onlookers. It is the risk-running racer on the track, not the hot-dog-eating grandstand sitter that gets the attention, the applause, the encouragement, and finally, the prize.

In today's world you must have the attention of people before you will get their business. Publicity is essential just to inform the world of existence.

Because the chance-taker gets the publicity, he also attracts support. Courageous people attract courageous people. Imaginative people attract imaginative people. Big thinkers are attracted to big thinkers. Be sure that big men and brave men are not attracted to the timid, dare-nothing, do-nothing person. Suddenly the glorified gambler finds that the best men, the biggest men, and the bravest men in the field are watching him! Surprising offers of help come from totally unsuspected sources. Great men are attracted to the struggling person who is bravely trying to do something wonderful. So unexpected offers of support make success possible. I have heard jealous impossibility thinkers say, "That firm was just lucky. Mr. Jones joined them and if it hadn't been for Mr. Jones they would have failed." But why did Mr. Jones join that team? Why didn't he join the jealous impossibility thinker's team? Because big people are inspired by and attracted to courageous people.

Be sure the safety-first thinkers, who move slowly, talk quietly, think small, and appear cautious, will give an impression of uncertainty and inner fear. No wonder they never inspire great men to join their team.

Because the chance-taker gets the spotlight and attracts support, he succeeds. And he wakes up one morning with the really big prize—self-confidence.

Self-confidence is security!

What is the spirit of security but a deep belief in yourself? What is insecurity but a lack of faith in one's own ability?

How do you give a person a sense of security? By giving him a chance to build faith in himself! Self-reliance and self-confidence are real security. When Communism collects people together and spares them from competition, protects them from the possibility of failure, and shelters them from the possibility of poverty, is it really offering security? It is perhaps eliminating the fear of poverty and starvation, but:

The absence of fear is no proof of courage.

Play-it-safe people may not be afraid. But this does not mean they are brave. What would happen if they had to face danger? Suddenly they would discover that they lacked real courage. Communism offers a counterfeit security, for real security is self-confidence.

The priceless gift of self-confidence can only be acquired when you succeed after being exposed to possible failure. Exposure to risk is the only route to real self-confidence. Self-confidence cannot be inherited. It must be earned by each individual, each generation, each new regime. And the only way to earn it is by taking a noble risk, an honorable chance, a glorified gamble. Self-confidence cannot be taught; it must be caught! And risk-running, chance-taking, is the only way to catch it. Mountain-moving faith succeeds in building self-confidence through chance-taking. Without self-confidence, faith will never muster and demonstrate mountain-moving power.

STEP 4. BEGINNING. You have a dream, you have ruled fear out of your thinking; now get going.

It is not enough to dream, desire, and dare. Mountain-moving faith now begins to act as if nothing is going to stop the dream from succeeding. We all know people who think great ideas and dream daring dreams, but never get started. Probably because as long as they postpone beginning, these big pretenders are still playing it safe.

Faith must move from the level of imagination into the level of conversation and then into the level of concrete organization. Get started! Do something!

It is my observation that real support for a cause never comes until we begin to exercise an aggressive faith.

God seldom performs a miracle until we try. And great faith involves going out on a limb where we run the risk of failure, possible embarrassment, and potential defeat. God does not allow us to face humiliating personal disaster if we have carefully and prayerfully ventured forth in a practical, human-need-filling, inspiring, exceptional faith-project! Someone said:

> **Even a turtle doesn't get ahead unless he sticks his neck out.**

One of the most helpful sentences I ever heard was from the lips of Professor Milton Hinga, a history professor at Hope College, Holland, Michigan. When he found out that none of the members of his history class had even started their term papers, he rose, paced the room, and said, "I am about to tell you the most important thing you will ever hear!"

Every eye focused upon him, waiting breathlessly for his great pronouncement. He spoke softly but firmly, "I don't care if you flunk. I don't care if you forget everything that I ever teach you in this class. But I never want you to forget this next sentence." After a dramatic pause he shouted out:

> **"Beginning is half done!"**

Do you have a good idea? Have you discussed it with knowledgeable people? And are you convinced that it is practical, inspiring, and exceptional? Do you dare to run the risks involved? Then get started today.

Too busy? Then maybe it is time to hire or ask somebody to help you.

This is often the beginning point. If you have a good idea, if it has passed the test of wise people, then it may pay you to hire the kind of a man who can get the project successfully off the ground. It may even pay to borrow the money to hire the men to successfully launch your venture. This may be the starting point for you.

Whatever you do—get started. Beginning is half done.

Fence-sitting faith doesn't even have the strength to move a mole hill. We can't expect God to move a mountain if we are not interested enough to get started.

> Grieve not for me,
> who am about to start
> a new adventure.
> Eager I stand,
> and ready to depart,
> me and my reckless, pioneering heart!
>   *Anon.*

STEP 5. EXPECTING. Not a few people think, talk, and actually begin, only to fail because their faith has not been deep enough to reach the deep expecting level of belief. They had enough faith to use their imagination. They had enough faith to enter into intelligent conversation with knowledgeable people. They had enough faith to actually establish an organization and begin their project. They had imagination, conversation, organization, but they lacked anticipation. After they got their venture launched, they began to worry, wonder, and doubt whether they would really ever succeed.

Dr. Norman Vincent Peale said, "Hope is the great power that can move you to success. Why? Because when a man expects to win, he does not hold anything back, but gives his project all that he's got. Most people fail not because they lack ability, intelligence, or opportunity, but they fail because they don't give it all they've got."

When you expect success, then you hold nothing back, but sink your last dime, spend your second-wind energy, and gamble your priceless reputation, confident that you'll make it. Such extreme dedication almost always leads to success, for when people know that you have given your wonderful idea all that you've got, they will march to your side and help you on to victory and success. One of the world's greatest religious statesmen moved mountains with this statement:

> **Attempt great things for God**
> **and expect great things from God.**

This does not mean that we will always reach our goals. It does mean that we shall reach our maximum height of potential effectiveness. Even if the maximum goal is not attained, the realized achievement will represent the ultimate of our abilities.

Do not be discouraged if you do not accomplish everything that you set out to accomplish.

Surely if you do not expect to succeed you will hold back your full power, investment, and enthusiasm. Immediately the kind of people who could help to move you on to victory begin to draw back. Your conservative and cautious attitude will reflect itself in an anxious look on your face that will disturb and discourage people from helping you.

There are two major reasons why people fail. Both stem from a lack of mountain-moving faith. Men who fail are often men who (1) are indecisive. They cannot make decisions swiftly and surely. The fast-moving opportunity is past before they decide—too late—to take hold. (2) Then some decisive people fail because, after making the decision, they fail to move forward with an expectant confidence. They grab the opportunity, only to lose nerve, get cold feet, and begin to wonder if they have done the right thing. They have gripped the plow but now they are looking back. Want to be a success? Develop the ability to appraise opportunities intelligently, seize opportunities swiftly, and promote these opportunities confidently.

STEP 6. AFFIRMING. Faith is affirming success before it comes. Faith is making claims to victory before it is achieved. This is very difficult to do, but most important.

Our instinctive sense of modesty and honesty tend to restrain us from making public statements of our anticipated success. We sense that any announcement of success before it is within our grasp is a sin of presumption and proud boasting. So we have a natural compulsion to say nothing, keep quiet, hope for the best, and when we have won we will make our joyous announcement.

Was St. Paul modest when he said, "I can do all things through Christ who strengthens me"? Was he exaggerating a bit? Was he literally truthful in this affirmation? Or was this an extreme exercise of mountain-moving faith talking?

The truth is that mountain-movers are people who boldly predict success. They know that "rats flee from the sinking ship." The know that nothing succeeds like success. They know that no one likes to follow a loser. They know they have to convey an image of winning or they will never gain the following they need to achieve their goal. So their bold prediction, their brash announcement, is not immodesty—nor is it dishonesty —nor is it cocky pride—it is FAITH IN DEPTH! It is faith that dares to take the sixth step.

Affirming—this is enthusiasm-generating faith. Great affirmations heighten the sense of expectancy and generate great enthusiasm.

Affirm success and you will visualize yourself winning. When you imagine yourself winning then that mysterious force of enthusiasm suddenly surges through your being.

Because enthusiastic people are happy people, they are energetic and ambitious people.

So enthusiastic people are spirit-lifting, morale-boosting, talent-attracting, hope-generating people.

It's no wonder that affirmative people magnetically attract to themselves gifted people who generously offer their talent, time, or treasure to make the exciting dream come true.

"Tell people confidently that you are going to win," I advised a young man running for office. "But what if I lose? What would I say then?" My answer was swift: "If you lose you can walk right up to them and say, 'Well, at least I had the faith that I was going to win!' Have you ever seen anyone win public office when he did not predict victory?"

It's a cinch—few men can move mountains all by themselves. And you will never attract or inspire people to help you unless you can offer them strong hope of ultimate success.

Is your faith deep enough to predict success before it is within your grasp?

STEP 7. WAITING. The kind of faith that moves mountains is a faith that has great waiting-power.

You have left the shallows, the water has gone over your head, you have taken the great plunge, you can no longer feel bottom beneath your feet, but you have not yet started to swim. This is the sweating phase of faith.

In every development there is a stage where you've thought it, started it, expected it, and affirmed it. Now you've passed the point of no return but cannot yet understand how ultimate success will be yours. Great and unexpected problems assault you. But you cannot back down, you cannot run away, you can only keep going and hope for the best.

Waiting—this is faith in deep waters. Almost every venture goes through a period of time when problems are overwhelming. This is the time to remind yourself that mountain-moving faith is faith with hold-the-line power.

How often I have been asked by discouraged people, "Reverend, I have prayed, but it doesn't seem to work for me. I have tried to believe in God, but it doesn't seem to help me. What's wrong with my faith?" In almost every instance I have to advise them that there is one vital ingredient missing in their faith. And that dynamic ingredient is patience.

> **Faith is patience!**

Men who really succeed are men who know that every project goes through phases when there is nothing to do but wait. The danger is that we may be tempted in this dreary time to quit.

Nine years ago I shared my dream of a church with a wise friend and asked for his advice. He said to me, "Well, Bob, it is a great idea. Probably all you can do at the moment is wait and let the thing evolve quite naturally." It was sane, sound, and sensible advice. I shall never forget the way he rolled out the word "evolve." There are times in a project, in a problem, in a goal, when there is nothing that we can do except wait.

This is especially true when we have experienced what may appear to be a failure or a costly setback. Successful people are men who refuse to believe in defeat. Their infinite patience generates fantastic bounce-back ability. Where the average individual would quit, the POSSIBILITY THINKER bounces back, confident that somehow, some way, sometime, a new opportunity will come along to pull him up and on to success.

Facing a tough time in your own life or business? If you have a patience-empowered faith, you will master that mountainous problem and you will win out. Time has a way of proving that what looks like a setback is really good fortune wearing a false mask.

Mountain-moving faith is faith with hold-the-line power when powerful pressures mount to defeat us.

Great faith is simply faith that will not quit.

If you simply cannot hang on any longer, then you may be ready for the deepest level of faith. For there are times when faith is—surrendering.

STEP 8. ACCEPTING. (Sometimes referred to as SURRENDERING.)

We all face situations when our mountain does not budge, in spite of all we do.

Then, it seems to me, the only thing we can do is offer that profound prayer of faith first offered by Jesus Christ. When death by crucifixion seemed imminent, He offered this faith-packed prayer: "My Father, all things are possible unto Thee. Nevertheless, not my will, but Thine be done." "Thy will be done" towers above all human utterances as the supreme statement of faith on the deepest level!

Mountain-moving faith is surrendering—letting go and letting God take over. "Thy will be done" is unquestionably the ultimate declaration of faith that can possibly fall from the lips of a human being.

This may be what's lacking in your faith if your mountain will not move. If, in spite of all that you are doing, your mountain will not move, then I suggest you try this miracle-generating prayer: "Thy will be done."

Recently a handsome young husband lost his wife. We failed in our efforts to help him overcome the mountain of grief that cast a black shadow of despair over his soul. Then came the day of the funeral. I prayed silently for him. After everyone had left the chapel, the grief-stricken husband and I stood alone at the casket. Then the miracle happened. Looking up with tearful face, he prayed, "Lord, I give her back to you." His faith reached mountainous heights. He stood tall and straight again! As he regained an amazing composure he looked at me and said, "She's in good hands now." And he walked forthrightly and strongly away. He had surrendered her to God. In surrendering, his faith found the power to move the mountain of grief. And the sunshine of warm peace fell into his mind.

How can you surrender your dreams, or your problems, to God? I can only tell you what has been helpful to me. The longer I study human life the more I realize that only God knows what's good and what's bad for us. One of my favorite stories is the classic story of the Chinese who had one horse and one son. One day his horse broke out of the corral and fled to the freedom of the hills. The neighbors came around that night and chattered, "Your horse got out? What bad luck!" "Why," the old Chinese said, "How do you know it's bad luck?" Sure enough, the next night the horse came back to his familiar corral for his usual feeding and watering, leading twelve wild stallions with him! The farmer's son saw the thirteen horses in the corral, slipped out and locked the gate. Suddenly he had thirteen horses instead of none. The neighbors heard the good news and came chattering to the farmer, "Oh, you have thirteen horses! What good luck!" And the old Chinese answered, "How do you know that's good luck?"

Some days later his strong young son was trying to break one of the wild stallions only to be thrown off and break a leg. The neighbors came back that night and passed another hasty judgment: "Your son broke his leg? What bad luck!" And the wise father answered again, "How do you know it's bad luck?" Sure enough, a few days later a Chinese war lord came through town and conscripted every able-bodied young man, taking them off to war, never to return again. But the young man was saved because of his broken leg. Only God knows what's good for us and what's bad for us.

"All things work together for good to those that love God." When we learn this lesson, then it becomes possible for us to pray the surrendering prayer of deepest faith, "Thy will be done."

If your mountain will not move, surrender it to God. He will either move it or show you how you can turn it into a mine or a monument.

"I'm going to have another baby. Maybe it will be the girl we've always wanted. Our four boys are so excited." It was Sara Rasmussen calling my wife. "You know," she went on, "we almost gave up hope of having another child." Laughing, she added, "We are practicing possibility thinking. It's just possible that we might have a daughter."

The ladies of the church excitedly planned a shower for Sara. "Think pink," the girls were told when they were invited to the party. When the surprised mother-to-be stepped into the room she saw pink flowers, pink ribbons, and all packages wrapped in pink paper.

Christmas music filled the air a few weeks later when her husband, Norm, called excitedly with the good news. "We have our daughter! We're naming her Leah. Both mother and daughter are feeling fine."

Arvella, my wife, answered the phone when Norm

called again two weeks later. This time his words came slowly and sadly. "The doctor brought us terrible news today. Leah is a Mongoloid. She may not live for more than a few years."

I called at the home. Sara answered the doorbell. She managed a brave smile under moist eyes. We sat down together. We prayed the prayer of acceptance: "Oh God, give us the courage to change those things that can be changed, the faith to accept those things that cannot be changed, and the wisdom to know the difference. Thy will be done. Amen."

I reminded Sara of Dale Evans and Roy Rogers: how God brought into their life a little baby who was destined to be an exceptional child like Leah; how this little one died some years later and how Dale summed it up in a book entitled *Angel Unawares*.

So when people advised Sara and Norm to place Leah in a special home, they prayed for guidance and told me their decision. "It would be the right decision for some families. But we are strong and our boys love the baby so. We know God wants her to stay right here in our own home where we can all love her."

That was eight years ago. Last week my wife received another call from Sara. "How are you, Sara? How's Leah?" The vibrant voice of a busy homemaker answered, "Leah's fine. You know I have four now." "Four? What do you mean?" Mrs. Schuller asked. "Well, we found three other exceptional children like Leah whose parents could not or would not take care of them. They are foster children, you see. I've decided to make a career of being a love-sharing homemaker. So we have taken these other children into our home. Leah just loves them. She isn't lonely any more. We have never been happier."

When I asked Norm if I might share their story with my readers, he answered, "Yes, and tell them there are beautiful possibilities for love and joy in every situation God allows to come our way. We don't *love* Leah more than the four boys, but we *enjoy* her more. You see, we have completely accepted Leah as a person. We expect her to be difficult at times so we are not upset by her difficult days. We don't expect her to be perfect. So we love her as she is—faults and all! Ever since we prayed 'Thy will be done' she has been one of the richest blessings of our lives."

Mountain-moving faith is

1. Dreaming
2. Desiring
3. Daring
4. Beginning
5. Expecting
6. Affirming
7. Waiting
8. Accepting

How do you get that kind of faith?

By getting acquainted with the GREATEST POSSIBILITY THINKER WHO EVER LIVED.

XIV

THE GREATEST POSSIBILITY THINKER WHO EVER LIVED

All the odds were against His ever being a POSSIBILITY THINKER.

In the first place He was a Jew. And the world was

jealous of the Jews. He didn't stand a chance. Especially since He was living behind the "Roman Curtain." He was a Nazarene. Even the "high class" Jews in Jerusalem looked down on a Nazarene from Galilee! Poor fellow, He just happened to be raised on the wrong side of the tracks. Everyone knew that Nazareth was the slummiest, sleaziest town in the whole land. It was the crossroads of world traffic and that meant wickedness. "Can anything good come out of Nazareth?" the snobbish people asked.

His father was a simple laborer. As a result He grew up in poverty. He had to work day and night to raise the money to pay His taxes. He never owned a home of His own. He said once, "Foxes have holes, birds of the air have nests, but the Son of Man has no place to call his own." Yet it didn't seem to dampen His enthusiasm for life one bit.

The miracle of His life was that He never once was infected with the contagious mental condition we call IMPOSSIBILITY THINKING. By nature He should have had every reason under the sun to become an impossibility thinker.

Moreover, He might have complained that He never had any really great opportunities. He never did have a chance to visit the great cities—Alexandria, Athens, Rome. He was in Jerusalem once when He was a boy. He visited the Temple. It impressed Him very much. He impressed the rabbis, too.

To top it all, He had no "connections." He just didn't know the right people. He couldn't impress people by dropping big names. He couldn't be a namedropper if He wanted to be. (Except to say that He and the Almighty were very good friends.) What kind of people was He attracted to? Not to the VIPs. Not to the lords of industry, politics, commerce, society, government, education, or religion.

What kind of people was He attracted to? To any person who could think big, believe big, and imagine big beautiful dreams.

> A fisherman who was able to believe that he could be a somebody.

> A diseased woman who dared to believe that she could be healed.

> A whore who dared to think that she could be a lady.

> A crooked politician who dared to believe that he could recover his lost dignity.

Why was He attracted to this kind of people? Because these were the only kind He could help! And these were the only kind of people who could help Him. He wanted to accomplish the impossible. He wanted to change the world. He believed that if He got the right men with the right spirit, He could succeed in changing the world. But they had to be POSSIBILITY THINKERS.

He tried to make greater POSSIBILITY THINKERS out of them: "If you have faith as a grain of mustard seed you can say to this mountain move, and it will move and nothing will be impossible to you."

"You can do anything, men, if you don't try to do it all alone. No man is an Island. God is in me and God can be in you too. You need God. A vine can't bear fruit if it is cut from the branch. You are children of God. You are God's branches in this world. You can live fruitful lives. But don't try to cut yourself off from His power. He is the root. You are the branches."

"*Without me you can do nothing,*" He said. And they really believed it when He said to them, "*You are the light of the world. You are the salt of the earth.*" He never did call them "sinners." He saw great possibilities in each of these men. How He tried to give them the sense of self-worth and dignity that they deserved! After all, they were human beings, descendants of God.

Yes, He could have been an *impossibility thinker.* For He never had much time to really do anything worthwhile. They killed Him when He was only thirty-three years old. So He died. Unmarried. Childless. Penniless. The Romans who hammered Him to the Cross threw dice to determine who could have His robe. When that was settled, there was nothing more. The crowd went home. He was dead now. But even this death was to Him His great opportunity! What a POSSIBILITY THINKER! "I, if I be lifted up, will draw all men unto me," He had said.

Yes, everything was an opportunity for Him! When He found himself with His hands hammered to a wooden cross he turned his crucifixion into a wonderful opportunity to dramatically tell all the world for all time that

---

there is no sin that God cannot forgive.

So He prayed, "Father, forgive them; for they know not what they do." And the cross has become a joyous symbol to remind the world that if God can forgive this depraved torture of an innocent Christ, He can forgive any sin. After He died some friends tenderly lifted Him down, gently wrapped His naked body, and put Him in a borrowed tomb.

"That's that!" thought the crowd which had finished its bloody deed. "Good riddance," thought His enemies. He had enemies. One evil that He could not tolerate was "insincere religion." He hit that hard and it got Him into trouble.

The crosses were taken down. Drifting sand would soon fill the holes. His body was dead and so was His "big idea," grandiose dream, and exaggerated talk. His followers were scattered. They were, frankly, scared stiff. Would they be next? No movement could be more obviously dead than His movement on that day. For He died. Leaving no manuscripts. No corporation. No property. No headquarters. Only a big idea that any man can do almost anything if he lives close to God and has enough faith.

This was His big idea.

And it seemed like His death proved Him wrong. But then something happened.

Whatever it was, His crushed, defeated, broken teammates suddenly were inflamed with a greater faith than any band of human beings in the history of the human race has ever displayed.

For He appeared to them. Alive again!

This great POSSIBILITY THINKER!

"Of course there is a God! I saw Him!"

"Of course there is life after death! I have been there to give the answer once and for all!"

"Of course God hears and answers prayers!"

"Of course you can go out and change the world! All of this is possible!"

This was what He came back to tell them. And these cowardly followers became the bravest men history has ever seen. They came out of hiding and into the streets. One thing is sure, they were positive that they had seen their Teacher alive again. All were so positive of it that whereas they were too scared to even show their faces one day, they were out preaching from the street corners not many days later. Not caring at all if they were killed themselves. "You people are drunk," someone said.

"Hardly, friend," they answered. "The truth is, this Christ who was killed is still alive! We saw Him. We talked to Him."

And these impossibility thinkers finally became the world's greatest POSSIBILITY THINKERS. Nothing could stop them. Nothing could keep them from succeeding. The spirit of their POSSIBILITY-THINKING Master had at last completely caught hold of them. And they were changed men.

The inspiring history of the Jewish people has stories of many brave, brilliant, and valiant men. But this band of God-inspired Jews has never been surpassed for courage, confidence, and determination.

For now at last they were overpowered by His living Spirit! His last word was, "Go, now, into the whole world, and preach this gospel to every creature. Begin here in Jerusalem. Then unto the uttermost parts of the world."

If they could have understood modern terminology He might have said, "I expect to have branch offices someday in London, Berlin, Paris, Rome, Tokyo, Rio de Janeiro, New York, Chicago, and Los Angeles."

What a big thinker! What a grand design! What a way to conquer the world! The world's greatest POSSIBILITY THINKER!

They didn't realize it but this POSSIBILITY THINKER was about to solve His biggest problem. For He had one big problem on this earth. It seemed like an "impossible problem." He could only be one place at a time.

Someone said to me recently, "It's too bad He isn't around today. We could sure use Him." And they added sadly, "Why did He have to die anyway?"

"Die? He isn't dead," I answered. "It seems to me that His Spirit is very, very much alive today."

"He just got rid of His body," I suggested. Adding, "That was the biggest problem He faced, you know. He had a body so He could only be one place at a time. While He was in the north, He should have been in the south too. I'm sure He must have thought many times, 'I wish I had a million bodies. A million hearts. A million tongues. Two million hands. I wish I could be at a million places at the same time.'"

So he conceived of the brilliant scheme of getting His body out of the way, and sending His living holy Spirit into the thinking brains of millions of people of every race, in every city, in every country, in the whole world! His way of getting to a million places at the same time!

Guess what? He is alive this very moment sending His messages into the minds of men. Your brain was deliberately designed to pick up God's spiritual signals in the form of ideas, impulses, and moods. Christ is busy this very moment sending out a message to you. It takes the form of a "possibility thought" in your mind. Listen to it! Respond to it! And Christ can live in you!

Jesus Christ would love to be wherever you are. Christ can be there by coming into your thoughts, feelings, and actions. Let Christ come into your total being and

- *Words will come out of you*
  that will shock you.
  "Did I say that?" you will ask.

- *Ideas will shoot into your mind*
  that will amaze you.
  "Did I think of that?" you will ask.

- *Feelings will rise strongly within you*
  to care about people you didn't care about before.
  "That's not like me," you will confess.

- *Impulses will suddenly stir within you*
  to help the unfortunate and
  to change your own bad habits,
  and you will begin to realize that
  CHRIST IS ACTUALLY LIVING IN YOU!

And you will say, as another famous Jew said centuries ago, "I can do all things through Christ who strengthens me." Of course! Christ keeps sending strong possibility thoughts. In the face of overwhelming obstacles we "get a bright idea." We just cannot be defeated when we are in contact with this great living soul. We see opportunities all around us. Always. All the days of our life. "If any man is in Christ, he becomes a new creature. Old things are passed away, behold! All things are become new."

There are millions of people like this all over the world. They are Christ-possessed people. Truly Jesus Christ is more alive today than he was two thousand years ago.

So Christ is living and working in this world.

He was living in the minds of the first American astronauts spinning in space.

Using the thinking minds and feeling hearts and strong wills of good men and women, He is teaching, healing, inventing, negotiating, forgiving, reassuring.

Wherever you are and whatever you do—if you have any contact at all with any other living human beings—you can be sure that Christ can use you and wants to live another life reincarnated within you. That is the supreme possibility of human life.

Christ has no hands but our hands to do His work today.
He has no feet but our feet to lead men on the way.

He has no tongues but our tongues to tell men how He died.
He has no help but our help to bring men to His side.

XV

NOW—SUCCEED AS A POSSIBILITY THINKER

Now you have learned how to succeed if you will:

STOP   the self-deceiving and self-defeating habit
          of defending your mistakes,
          rationalizing your sins,
          making excuses for your failures, and
          whitewashing your errors of judgment.

LOOK   deeply into yourself and your situation
          and see the slumbering possibilities
          that wait to be awakened.

LISTEN   to constructive criticism,
          sensible advice, and
          honest counsel that
          serious and sincere friends have been trying
          for years to communicate to you.

I

NOW—SEE AND SEIZE THE POSSIBILITIES WITHIN YOURSELF

Use possibility thinking to overcome your feelings of inferiority, inadequacy, and unimportance. Achieve self-confidence and surprise yourself and those around you. Learn to live with yourself and like it. Here's how:

1. UNDERSTAND YOURSELF and the people around you. Don't be fooled. People are not as interested in your appearance as they are in your personality. You can't change your looks but you can change your personality.

2. DEHYPNOTIZE YOURSELF. For many years you have probably been telling yourself that you are either inadequate, inferior, unattractive, ineffective, untalented, unintelligent, or lacking in confidence, charm, grace, and poise until you have made yourself believe all these negative lies! If these are your thoughts—change them.

3. DEHYPNOTIZE YOURSELF BY REHYPNOTIZING YOURSELF through powerful God-filled affirmations: "I can do all things through Christ who strengthens me."

4. ACCEPT YOURSELF. Stop fighting your background. Stop hating your past. No matter where you were born, what color your skin, what accent your speech, God made you the way you are because He wanted you to be different! Distinctive! He likes what He created. Why don't you?

5. IMPROVE YOURSELF. Nothing bolsters self-esteem more than self-improvement. Read some mind-stretching matter every week. Improve your knowledge, and your understanding of people and things. In short, keep growing. Keep expanding your interests. You are not old until you decide to quit growing. Staleness brings self-dislike.

6. EXCEL AT SOMETHING. When we feel we are average or mediocre, or not really good at some specific activity, we suffer from self-depreciation. Try to excel at something—like being the most thoughtful person in the block, or the friendliest, sweetest, or most understanding person in the group wherein you move. You can excel in some area if you try.

7. CONNECT YOURSELF to something bigger than yourself. Some people do this by joining a club or organization. That's good. Connect yourself with the Church

and you will have that wonderful feeling of belonging to the group where God is living and working.

8. SHARE YOURSELF with others. Build friendships in depth. In today's world few people have time for any deep friendships. We know hundreds of people in a shallow and safe way. Give yourself deeply to a few people with whom you share some interests. And make sure that Jesus Christ is your closest, deepest, most intimate friend.

9. NOW—FORGET YOURSELF. The secret of self-respect is in self-forgetfulness. Give yourself in love and service and you'll have no time to get sick with "ingrown thinking."

II

DETECT AND DEVELOP THE POSSIBILITIES WITHIN EVERY CONSTRUCTIVE IDEA

You must understand that you are not being intelligent when you slam the door shut on a suggestion until you have carefully thought through the possibilities that may lie within the proposal. Discipline yourself to think positively about every idea. Here's how:

1. LISTEN CAREFULLY. Keep an open mind until the person has finished explaining his proposal.

2. DISTRUST your first negative reaction—it is likely to be defensive thinking on your part. It may even be prejudice-thinking.

3. GUARD AGAINST THE TENDENCY TO CLOSE YOUR MIND to the potential value in the idea because it interferes with your plans.

4. BE SLOW to cast an unqualified "No" vote to an idea that has any value whatever.

5. REMIND YOURSELF that there are objectionable aspects to almost every constructive proposal.

6. DON'T SLAM THE DOOR SHUT on an idea that has some constructive content just because you don't like it,

you don't think it can work, or you see something wrong with it.

7. LOOK FOR THE POSITIVE POSSIBILITIES IN THE PROPOSAL. Immediately sift and lift the profit potential from the proposal. If you can't see any good at all, ask yourself if you are still thinking like an impossibility thinker.

8. Now LOOK FOR POSSIBLE WAYS TO HANDLE the disagreeable, undesirable, or hazardous features in the positive idea. Find people smarter than yourself to come up with possible ways to *isolate, eliminate, insulate, neutralize,* or *sublimate* the unpleasant parts of the proposal.

9. Now IMAGINE MANY WAYS AND MEANS to capitalize on the value potential in the positive proposal.

NEVER, through all this mental maneuvering, will you allow yourself to think or believe that anything is impossible. Result? You will take ideas that others rashly discard as too dangerous, costly, or worthless and you will turn these ideas into great opportunities.

III

SPOT AND SEIZE THE POSSIBILITIES WITHIN THOSE OPPORTUNITIES AROUND YOU

Use possibility thinking to turn your opportunities into real successes. Here's how to go about it:

1. REJECT your inclination to inferiority thinking. Instead of being frightened by the prospect of failure, face your big chance with reinforcing self-confidence. Reject impossibility thoughts like "I'm not smart enough" or "I don't know the right people" or "I don't have the right connection" or "I don't have the talent" or "I'm handicapped."

2. INJECT confidence-generating thoughts into your mind

like "I can do all things through Christ who strengthens me," "All things are possible if I will believe," "If I have faith as a grain of mustard seed I can say to this mountain move and nothing is impossible for me."

3. SELECT your immediate and long-range goals. Then make an exhaustive list of the many possible ways in which you could possibly succeed in reaching your desired objective.

4. PROJECT your plan. Begin. Make a public announcement. Tell enough people until your honor will not let you quit. You know that the hardest part of the journey is the first step.

5. COLLECT the time, money, energy, and brain power to do the job. Surround yourself with trusted and talented associates.

6. EXPECT to succeed. Throw everything you have into it. Give your whole heart to your dream.

Refuse to believe in defeat and you will turn your opportunity into a profitable and exciting enterprise.

IV

FACE AND FIND THE POSITIVE POSSIBILITIES IN YOUR PROBLEM

Keep a strong possibility posture as you confront your problem with creative poise. You will use possibility thinking to:

1. REMIND YOURSELF that every problem is an unfilled need.

2. REMEMBER THAT SUCCESS IS FINDING A NEED AND FILLING IT.

3. VIEW your problem as an opportunity in disguise.

4. WELCOME your problem as a guideline or challenge.

5. LOOK FOR AND FIND SOMEONE SOMEWHERE who can help you solve or sublimate this problem.

If you live near the ocean, watch the waves roll in. You may see a timid swimmer who, spotting a great wave rising, panics, turns, and runs, only to be overcome by the rushing mountain of water and sent tumbling and sputtering in the surf. Now watch the surfer. He looks for and sees the savage wave swelling. He welcomes the wave with the spirit of Caleb, "Give me a mountain!" He is poised with a surfboard in his hands. As the rising, racing wave reaches full crest this possibility thinker mounts the liquid mountain and is lifted high and carried far!

Face your problems with creative poise and you will never be defeated.

V

TRY TO FIND CONSTRUCTIVE POSSIBILITIES IN A PERSONAL HEARTBREAKING EXPERIENCE

How do possibility thinkers come alive again after undergoing a personal tragedy? Believe me, I have, as a pastor, seen hundreds of courageous people turn their tragedy into an inspiring experience. Here's how:

1. STEEL YOURSELF AGAINST SELF-PITY. Who do you think you are to be spared this heartbreak? God has not promised "skies always blue, flower-strewn pathways all our lives through." Self-pity will only kill your own spirit.

2. DON'T TORTURE YOURSELF WITH GUILT. There is always guilt mixed in with grief. This is natural. But it is harmful. Don't hurt yourself still more by blaming yourself. Blaming yourself won't help anyone and it will hurt you and others as well. If you are honestly guilty, turn it over in deep prayer to Christ. He specializes in forgiveness. That's what makes the cross

a beautiful symbol to Christians. Now forgive yourself.

3. WITH A COOL HEAD REMIND YOURSELF THAT THIS TRAGEDY WILL "MAKE ME A WORSE PERSON IF I LET IT." Trouble never leaves you where it found you. It will leave you a more bitter, cynical, hard, and cold person if that's what you want. But use your head and remind yourself that this will only compound your misery. For no cynical, bitter person is happy. Brace yourself against the destructive emotional re-action called bitterness. Don't make matters worse for yourself and others.

4. AFFIRM TO YOURSELF—OUT LOUD—"I WILL LET THIS TRAGEDY MAKE ME INTO A BETTER PERSON." And it will. You will become a far more sensitive, sympa-thetic, and comforting person to those around you. "In love's service only broken hearts will do." This tragedy holds the possibilities of making you a sweeter, lovelier, more beautiful and compassionate person.

5. THINK—THIS TRAGEDY WILL EITHER DRAW YOU CLOSER TO GOD OR DRIVE YOU FARTHER FROM GOD. A Great Hebrew prophet, Elijah, found faith in sorrow: "In the year that King Uzziah died, I saw the Lord," the prophet wrote. Many people will report that in their time of deepest heartache they had their richest encounter with the living God.

Let your troubles turn you closer to God. Draw close to Christ. He lives, He loves, He leads, He lifts!

You will find the joy that comes to those who love deeply because they have been hurt deeply.

You will never be crushed by the adversities of life. Possibility thinking will make your life an inspiration and a triumph!

A Lifetime of Answers...

JOVE INSPIRATION BOOKS

If they can do it, so can you.

But first find out *how* they did it.

Develop your success potential with these six books written by and about people who have discovered the secret of getting ahead. If you want more out of life, these books are for you!

__ 06305-4	**THE POSSIBLE DREAM** Charles Paul Conn	$2.95
__ 06306-2	**THE WINNER'S CIRCLE** Charles Paul Conn	$2.95
__ 07286-X	**THE WINNER'S EDGE** Dr. Denis Waitley	$2.95
__ 05870-0	**AN UNCOMMON FREEDOM** Charles Paul Conn	$2.95
__ 06272-4	**WITH NO FEAR OF FAILURE** Thomas J. Fatjo, Jr. and Keith Miller	$2.95

Prices may be slightly higher in Canada.

Available at your local bookstore or return this form to:

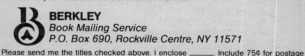

BERKLEY
Book Mailing Service
P.O. Box 690, Rockville Centre, NY 11571

Please send me the titles checked above. I enclose _____ Include 75¢ for postage and handling if one book is ordered; 25¢ per book for two or more not to exceed $1.75. California, Illinois, New York and Tennessee residents please add sales tax.

NAME _____

ADDRESS _____

CITY _____ STATE/ZIP _____

(allow six weeks for delivery)   **158**